Leadership
Directions
from Moses

LEADERSHIP DIRECTIONS
from Moses

On the Way to a Promised Land

OLU BROWN

Abingdon Press
Nashville

LEADERSHIP DIRECTIONS FROM MOSES:
ON THE WAY TO A PROMISED LAND

Copyright © 2017 by Abingdon Press

This book is printed on acid-free paper.

Library of Congress Cataloging-in-Publication Data.

Names: Brown, Olu, author.
Title: Leadership directions from Moses : on the way to a promised land / Olu Brown.
Description: Nashville : Abingdon Press, [2017] | Includes bibliographical references.
Identifiers: LCCN 2016055684 (print) | LCCN 2017026210 (ebook) | ISBN 9781501832543 (e-book) | ISBN 9781501832536 (pbk.)
Subjects: LCSH: Christian leadership. | Pastoral theology.
Classification: LCC BV652.1 (ebook) | LCC BV652.1 .B778 2017 (print) | DDC 253--dc23
LC record available at https://urldefense.proofpoint.com/v2/url?u=https-3A__lccn.loc.gov_2016055684&d=DwIFAg&c=_GnokDXYZpxapTjbCjzmOH7Lm2x2J46Ijwz6YxXCKeo&r=ox0wiE5wyqlD4NWBvXI_LEW57Ah1_xv-dTElReAYRyw&m=ei2ZmIhjfh0iOHE6QCnaUdOZoteoCk9H1zN-NWh71dc&s=CVIiTvHtBv6mlfcyKum6Iym1iRsUEvgLv5LE784jtC0&e=

17 18 19 20 21 22 23 24 25 26—10 9 8 7 6 5 4 3 2 1

MANUFACTURED IN THE UNITED STATES OF AMERICA

I dedicate this book to my
daughter and son, Daya and Langston,
and to those seeking their promised land.

CONTENTS

INTRODUCTION

I t never fails. The best and most profound moments when I hear God's voice and direction are during my personal devotional time. On most occasions this takes place during the early morning hours when my family is still asleep. On other occasions I hear God as I am on the run, stealing a moment or two to center my thoughts, trying to hear God's voice for a right-now word of hope and direction. Deep down, I know my personal devotion time is what God desires from me, but I don't find it easy to always settle my body, mind, and soul. Yet whenever I am reluctant to spend quality quiet time with God, I feel as though I am missing something spectacular.

A few years ago, I remember stumbling across something spectacular on a day that I am glad I did not neglect my devotional time. I happened to notice the text in Numbers 32 where the verses revealed a scene when the Israelites sojourned to the promised land with Moses leading them as their chief elder and guide. This scene was between Moses and the two tribes of Gad and Reuben, who requested to remain in the wilderness and not live in the land of promise with their fellow Israelites. Numbers 32:5 reveals their stunning proposal to Moses: "If you approve our request, give this land to your servants as property."

Looking back now on that day a few years ago, I know that I didn't stumble upon this text by chance. I am sure that the spirit of God led me to it. I will forever be grateful and honored to be able to see and know Numbers 32 in a new and dynamic way. Have you ever had a moment when a passage in the Bible spoke to you differently—a time when although you had read or heard the text before, something was different this particular time? If we are not careful in our Bible reading, we may miss the diamonds in the rough that God has in store for us through the words and pages of the sacred text. God is always speaking and giving us direction and hope, even in the midst of our most confusing and broken moments. It is essential to hear and understand God's voice and direction in leadership. Leaders are responsible for others, and it is important for them to know that there is a greater source of direction beyond themselves pointing those they are leading in the right direction. Being a leader can be difficult. We leaders, more than anyone, need direction and correction. We are often navigating unfamiliar territory, and it is quite easy to become caught up in the difficulty and pressures of our responsibilities. Remembering that God is always speaking and giving us direction and hope becomes our lifeline for our survival as well as for the communities and organizations we lead.

The day I read Numbers 32 in my devotional time, it spoke to me as a leader, giving me a new insight and direction for my journey. The text helped me to correct my course, showing me new possibilities within God's call on my life. This text revealed an interesting twist and turn within the story of Moses leading the children of Israel from bondage to freedom. Suddenly a well-planned trip threatened to veer drastically off course as two of the tribes of Israel, the Reubenites and Gadites, asked for permission to stay in the wilderness. Although the whole community of Israel had signed up to go to the land flowing with milk and honey, the Reubenites and the Gadites shifted their itinerary and asked to be released from their original faith agreement. Have you ever experienced a potential "derailment" moment like this in your life when in one moment or two the entire plan could potentially be shifted in a different direction? Moses was not alone in this instance because throughout history most leaders and great movements of God have faced the reality of derailment. Technically, your movement, organization, church, or group hasn't accomplished much unless you've been threatened with one or two threats of derailment.

Think about the weight of their request to Moses—to stay in the place that was not promised to them and wasn't God's ultimate endgame for the future of Moses and the Israelites. Can you imagine? After more than nine years of leading a new church and more than twenty-one years of preaching the good news, I can say, "Yes, I can imagine a glimpse of the incredible weight that Moses experienced." On the journey of life, we face moments when we realize that our promise may not be the same promise as that of the crowd or of those whom we admire the most. God gives us permission to choose our own promises and claim hold of our own destinies. Often families experience these realities as high school–age teenagers begin to become more aware of who they are and may select a path outside of the chosen path of the family. These can be difficult situations to navigate because no one wants to disappoint his or her parent or loved one. The same is true in our work lives and friendships. As humans we have a deep and abiding "pleasing mechanism" that always wants to please and never disappoint. I believe deep down the Reubenites and Gadites wanted to please Moses and truly didn't want to disappoint their fellow Israelites. But over time their own sense of destiny overpowered their desire to please and they chose their own promise—the promise to stay while Moses and the others moved forward.

Now you have a quick description of how I felt when I read Numbers 32 and why I wrote this book. This book is not only about how the Israelites claimed their promise, but it's about their journey along the way.

Leadership Directions from Moses is for those of you who consider yourselves to be both leaders and chasers of dreams and promises. Somehow along the way, like Moses and the Israelites, you hit roadblocks and speed bumps. You may doubt your promise, and those traveling with you may choose their own paths, but somehow and someway you press on with what you have and who you are. This book is written for people like Moses, as well as people like the Reubenites and the Gadites. It is for people who answer the phone, read the text, or open the e-mail and the message they receive literally causes their hearts to skip a beat. In one moment the news communicated is that the game is changing whether you like it or not. *Leadership Directions from Moses* is also for the person who has to be the "bad" guy or girl and deliver the breaking news of a sudden departure. This book is for the people who heard God tell them that they have a great future, but seem never to reach the promised land. It is for people who had to say goodbye to someone they loved along the way, wipe away their tears, and press forward to their goals. This book is for those who signed up for what they thought was the journey of a lifetime, but somewhere on the ride to their future, they hit the brakes and got off the road leading to God's promise for them. *Leadership Directions from Moses* is for you and for me, for all of us who look at the stars at night, searching for place and space, wondering if we will ever get there and what we will have to face along the safari of life.

During a trip to Kenya, I was blessed to go on a safari. I learned the meaning of *safari* is "journey." Like the Israelites' and Moses's, our lives are full of safari experiences that lead us to our own promises in God. However, it is "the stuff" of the journey, the details of what happens along the way, that teaches us the most about life, ourselves, and God. Whether the promise God has given you is to the left or the right, you are on a journey and it is up to you to embrace the safari experience as you take the journey of life.

Let's return to this story in the text at a point of deep dialogue, a point of mid-conversation between Moses and the tribes of Reuben and Gad. These two tribes are unknowingly—or knowingly—upsetting the balance and productivity of their community. Great teams and leaders always experience these moments when the delicately maintained balance of hopes and plans seems to shift as pieces and people fall out of line, veering in opposite directions. They can seem to be lost forever, if not reorganized quickly. Numbers 32 teaches us that all can be saved through the grace of God.

Chapter 1

BEGINNINGS

Moses was taking a brief leadership break on a rarely mild summer day, wonderfully cool and breezy, with no plans except to simply relax and enjoy time that was not committed to anything in particular. He'd decided to take advantage of a beautiful nearby water oasis by using the handcrafted fishing pole and personalized tackle box his wife, Zipporah, had given him for one of their wedding anniversaries. Moses was excited about taking some time for himself to enjoy one of his favorite pastimes and to reflect on the last few days.

> *What do you do to refresh yourself as a leader? "A study by a leading 'Christian think tank' has shown that stress and exhaustion in pastoral ministry causes as many as 70 percent of pastors to regularly consider leaving, and many of them actually quit."*[1]

As Moses was leaving his tent with his enviable fishing gear in tow, the leaders of the tribes of Reuben and Gad approached him. Moses noted the serious looks on their faces and immediately knew that his well-deserved break was coming to a really quick end. Isn't it funny how we can always tell by the ringtone, the text notification, or the incoming e-mail or voicemail that something serious—perhaps life-altering—is on the horizon?

Moses was familiar with life-altering moments, and he understood what it meant to have to adjust and shift quickly. His mother, Jochebed, taught him this lesson when she saved his life as described in Exodus 2, by placing him in the Nile River, hoping that he would be rescued by a caring family. Later in the same chapter, Moses experienced a significant life-shift when through his anger and immaturity he murdered an Egyptian. Having committed this crime, he ran for his life to Midian. As time passed, Moses transformed and began to live into the vision that God had for his life. He answered God's call to liberate his people from bondage and began to develop into the leader God knew he could be. All along the safari, Moses experienced life-altering moments and shifts. One of the most profound shifts came through his father-in-law, Jethro, who taught him to be less autocratic in his leadership and more democratic through delegation.

Moses's story is not unlike that of many leaders who have had to find their way through trial and error as they are leading, benefiting from those who were willing to mentor and guide them to the next level. Moses had been leading the people long enough to know when something was headed down the wrong path. Encountering the tribal leaders of Reuben and Gad reminded him of the way he felt when God surprised him in the wilderness, saying, "So get going. I'm sending you to Pharaoh to bring my people, the Israelites, out of Egypt" (Exod 3:10). Honestly, Moses somehow knew that his life would never be the same again. He'd been comfortable in Midian, thinking that he would live his life in the background, living down his past failures, including when he had allowed his anger to get the best of him. Being in the background of life seemed to be a suitable punishment for his crime. Moses was okay with inhabiting the part of the stage nearest the exit door. Why would God ask *him* to leave obscurity to do something so great and wonderful? How could God consider *him* to become known beyond his own lifetime, into eternity, to be revered by those who are God-followers? He experienced this same feeling when he was shaking in his boots, looking into the eyes of the most powerful person in the world, and demanding on behalf of God, "Let my people go so that they can hold a festival for [God] in the desert" (Exod 5:1).

This time, though, it wasn't God or Pharaoh whom Moses faced. He was facing the leaders of the Reubenites and the Gadites. Together, the Reubenite and Gadite tribes represented more than eighty thousand of the Israelites. Reuben was the firstborn son of Jacob and Leah. Gad was also a child of Jacob and Leah, but biblical scholars have documented less information about Gad. Like the men after whom these two tribes were named, these people were independent thinkers, always willing to risk it all for what they felt was best. Maybe you know a few Reubenites and Gadites in your circles and their passion for adventure and free will. I recall planting Impact Church in 2007 and being so sure about the people we wanted. As a matter of fact, these were the specific notes listed in our original vision documents about the people we wanted to reach each Sunday in our new church:

3

Description of the New Faith Community

The new faith community will attract people from all walks of life.

- Non-believers/pre-Christians who have had no prior connection to the Christian church.

- Believers in Christ who once were, but are no longer committed to the Christian faith.

- Committed Christians with the intention of helping them strengthen their faith and commitment to Christ.

- People of various races and cultures who are seeking a spiritual home.

- College students who are away from home.

- Homeless individuals who have no residence.[2]

Call it stupidity or prophecy, but we were positive about the types of people God would send our way when we started worship, only to awaken to the reality that the majority of those who showed up were off our grid. I believe this is good because we always need to have hearts big enough to receive those people we may not be looking for but God intends to show up. The Reubenites and Gadites were likely not atop Moses's list of best individual tribes. The good news is Moses stayed the course and balanced his desire for the type of people he imagined with the type of people God sent him to lead to the promise.

These two tribal leaders approached Moses because of their boldness and willingness to follow their passion. They were actually requesting to stay in the wilderness and claim the land they felt was best for them. This request startled Moses, as it would any leader, because never before had anyone asked Moses this question. From Moses's perspective, these leaders were actually deciding to settle for land that was not a part of God's promise to them. Did they really comprehend what they were risking? Moses knew this would be a defining moment in his leadership legacy.

Do you recall having an experience when you realized the next decision or action would be a defining leadership moment for you? Our church hosted an evening midweek worship experience for one year. As we reached the end of the year, I clearly knew the worship experience was not right for our church and was draining resources and many of our leaders knew that we needed to discontinue the evening midweek worship experience and face the reality and risk of disappointing those who supported the midweek experience. I am glad we decided to discontinue the evening midweek experience, because we knew not making this decision would set our church on a course of mediocrity due to choosing comfort over tough decisions.

As past feelings of change in the air elevated within him, Moses realized that he had long since given up on his hope for a beautiful day filled with relaxation. He promptly placed his fishing pole and tackle box to the side, inviting the leaders to join him in his tent. Once inside, he offered them a seat and small talk ensued. However, he knew in the back of his mind that something serious was brewing below the surface. Moses held off the serious talk for as long as he could, dreading it. Everyone sat with a sense of hesitation and trepidation as a thickness of unease filled the space. It was like the pause and chill felt right before authorities release breaking news that changes everyone's lives forever. Moses took in the silent emotions in the room that were so thick he could cut them with a knife. As much as he tried to hold them back, Moses stumbled through the first words that came out of his mouth. He said out loud what he had been thinking in his head: "Weeerrreee you . . . you, you just in the neighborhood or did you have something important to talk about?" Moses hadn't stumbled over his words like this since he'd told God he couldn't talk during his "call experience" to deliver the Israelites.

Many years had passed since Jethro, Moses's father-in-law, advised him about delegating responsibility so as not to burn out as a leader. Although he had listened to Jethro's wisdom in the past, this moment seemed different. He didn't have anyone to whom to delegate this matter. This issue was his to handle, and he felt the weight of the world on his shoulders. Yet he also felt he was in the right place, at the right time, having the right conversation with the tribal leaders. In this moment, he felt grounded and connected with the people he had led for many years and the God who had called him in the desert through a magnificent burning bush. Although he was a veteran leader by now, who had been tried by fire, a small part of him wondered if this was one of those times when he wished he had not invited these leaders into his space and perhaps should have told them to return at a better time. Dr. Sam Chand speaks of this in his book *Leadership Pain*.[3] We have a choice to postpone pain or charge into pain because change always causes pain. Sometimes, because our pain threshold is low, we neglect to face the impending pain and postpone the inevitable. Moses had endured and suffered a great amount of leadership pain on his journey, and I am grateful he raised his pain threshold as the two tribal leaders stood in his tent and he dug deep within his soul to withstand this next test.

The two tribal leaders paused and looked at Moses and then stared at each other as if they were both daring one to speak before the other. Finally, one of the leaders spoke up and with an unsure tone said, "Moses, we are grateful for you and your leadership."

Yep, this is a breaking news example that will forever change our lives. These two leaders were never the flattering type. Moses continued to brace himself, drawing strength from that place that still resided in his spirit from when he had confronted Pharaoh and lifted his staff to part the Red Sea. As Moses leaned forward to listen, one of his leaders started to speak again.

"Moses, we have been on this journey for a long time. It has truly been a great experience for our families. We have gotten over the idea that this will be a short journey and settled in to trust God with you. We have traveled to lands and met people that only existed in our dreams. We know it is truly because God has given our people favor and grace, even when we didn't deserve it. Although the journey has not been easy, we are grateful. Just the other day, my wife mentioned how much our family and resources have grown since we left Egypt and began the journey to the promised land. We can't imagine what the real promised land will be like. That's why we all feel so guilty for having complained in the old days, when God guided you to release us from bondage. I don't know what we were thinking. We are better off now than we were then."

Moses interrupted the leader mid-flattery to say, "Thank you, but you must be here to give me more than a thank-you and flattery. Please, why did you come to speak to me?"

The leader started again. "We came here today to ask for your permission . . ."

"My *permission*," Moses wondered. "For what???"

The leader continued . . .

Is there someone on the team asking for permission to leave but doesn't have the courage to leave? Think about your volunteers. Is there someone you feel is showing up but lacks energy, solution resources, and drive? He or she is a great person but may be burned out and too afraid to bow out. You may have to make a tough decision and ask this individual to leave or transition from a position because he or she may never take the initiative that the Reubenites and Gadites took and ask for permission to leave.

"Over the past few weeks our two tribes have been thinking about the many blessings we have received. We have been journeying through land and water that are appealing to us, right now. I know you keep telling us during our weekly leadership gatherings that the promised land flows with milk and honey, that we are just around the corner from the greatest blessings of our lives. Moses, last night we met with our tribes over dinner, and we had an intense conversation. We talked openly about where we have been and where we are going. Well, that is why we are here today. After looking at how much God has blessed our families and although we signed up for the promised land, we have decided to stay here in this part of the wilderness to build our permanent homes and plant crops in the soil, build our lives here. We believe in the promise that God gave you, but we sense that this land is the promise that God is giving to us. Moses, please forgive us and don't be angry. We came today to ask for your permission to stay. We came to say goodbye."

In that very moment Moses noticed the pieces of luggage from behind the robes of the leaders. *Permission? Their bags are already packed*, Moses realized. I remember reading the words of a pastor who mentioned the pain and reality of people who had left his church. Whether it is a church or business with repeat customers, people will come and go. It is shocking and surprising when people make a decision to leave, but the goal is to stay focused on the promise and not the loss along the way.

Moses knew even more that this was not an ordinary conversation. For a minute or two, Moses could not speak, not even stutter. He wondered how he had missed the signs, the remarks, and the slight suggestions along the way. He knew this meeting would be a defining moment in his leadership and spiritual journey. He knew this moment would recalibrate his life and the stories of the people he was leading. Although Moses's face had grown wrinkled with age and leadership, he was not so hardened that the tribal leaders could not still see what he felt on the inside, revealed by his facial expressions and the tears flowing down his dusty cheeks. By this time, he had begun to resemble more a regal grandfather than a powerful patriarch. The whole group paused, knowing this was a defining moment along their journeys as well. This pause seemed to be the longest one ever for them; they didn't know that the pause felt eternally long to Moses as well.

Once, in a session with a coach trained in helping others offer their best in moments of public speaking and dramatic presentations, I was told to "trust the pause." For those of you who speak publicly, the pause is probably not something you trust but something you avoid, because typically a pause means something has gone wrong and the worst is yet to come. Since that session I have reflected on the wisdom of the coach and have come to a point of being able to "trust the pause." For me the pause is not solely for the stage, but the pause is in life and relationship. If you are like me you want to quickly rush past the pause, but the pause is necessary because although uncomfortable, the pause, gives us time to catch our breath, recalibrate, and shift into a more positive future. Moses and the Reubenites and Gadites needed this uncomfortable pause because without it their past relationship would have been insignificant because no one pauses for insignificant relationships and circumstances. The longer the pause, the more significant the moment and relationship.

Take a moment to take a pause. This is difficult because you are running right now. Most of us suffer some type of trauma daily that may not be catastrophic but still traumatic. If you live in a large city and watch the morning news, you face trauma every morning as you watch the news reels of the fires, murders, and accidents. This moment for Moses and the Reubenites and Gadites was traumatic. The pause doesn't reduce the trauma but acknowledges the significance of the moment and helps all parties eventually move forward.

For a brief second, Moses felt a little faint with a knot building in his throat, preventing him from breathing easily or speaking with ease. For the first time in a long time, he became a little choked up and tried not to let his emotions get the best of him. Over the years his emotions had gotten the best of him. He was a murderer, literally broke the commandments, and struck a rock out of frustration with God's people. However, his emotions of sadness quickly shifted to anger as he thought about all that he had done for these two tribes—the number of times he'd prayed that God would bless them. Anger is a real and present emotion we all have that says we are human. Anyone who tells you he or she has never been angry or doesn't get angry is lying. Moses's anger was not different from the anger of any other person.

Some years ago, Jack Nicholson and Adam Sandler starred in a popular comedy titled *Anger Management*. In the movie, Sandler's character suffered from anger management issues and was ordered by the court to spend time with Nicholson's character, who was an anger management coach. In the end, the anger issues were overcome but not without a lot of intentional work. Specifically, for the anger to be resolved, the anger had to be revealed. Oftentimes we are given the impression that our leaders are perfect and that they should never be angry or afraid. I believe this is the worst advice any leader can live with because to be human is to experience both anger and fear. Moses became angry because he cared, and when we care, we feel. As his anger continued to boil, a sudden fear slipped into the equation—fear that other tribes might ask to stay in the wilderness as well and not journey with everyone into the promised land.

As a leader, I have often allowed anger to get the best of me and am ashamed to say that I have not handled anger well. Of course, I am not talking about an anger that if unchecked would be the catalyst for me harming someone or committing some other unfathomable crime. This anger is subtler—the anger of unresolved emotions, being rejected, not being selected, or failing to make a connection with someone. How do you manage anger, or does anger manage you? In life, there are few things we can control, but we can always control our responses to the things that happen to us. Hopefully you are working to control the powerful anger in your life that we all experience from time to time.

Moses feared that the other tribes would revolt and his leadership and vision would be challenged and compromised. So many emotions coursed through his body in these contracted moments in his tent with two of his tribal leaders. He felt as if the world had stopped turning and the eye of the universe focused on him alone. Moses began privately to reminisce about the time with God in the desert when he had heard God's call and promise clearly. The call had been to set God's people free. Although he had been afraid, he had heard God's call to deliver God's people. He had heard many words in his life up until that point, but no other messages had been as clear and powerful as the words from God at the burning bush.

When he was finally able to regain his composure and the deeply lodged knot in his throat had passed, Moses politely asked the two tribal leaders to give him some time to think about their request. They quickly agreed and exited the tent. Like Moses, we are faced with numerous requests that multiply our need for clarity in thought and sharp negotiation skills. The challenge is that we don't often have the time to think critically to make the wisest decisions and shift to overload mode. One mentor constantly reminds me to be careful to withhold decisions during moments of fatigue. Over the years, I have learned that it is always best to take time to think about the big decisions even if the requesting party is in a rush.

> *Maybe you have heard the saying "Don't let your emergency become my emergency." This is a very fitting directive because people will want to place their own rush on your life. This is okay if you don't mind rushing, but over time it becomes taxing. The answer to your leadership anxiety might be taking more time between big decisions and becoming more comfortable with saying "no" or "wait."*

As Moses pondered his decision alone in his tent, to his surprise, the two tribal leaders returned to talk to him again and secretly Moses wondered why they had returned so soon and didn't honor his request for time to think about the request. He thought he had been clear about needing time.

This time when the tribal leaders entered Moses's tent, they immediately became concerned because Moses's demeanor had changed. They wondered if he was okay. They didn't mean to cause any additional stress in his life or to break his heart. From their perspective, they weren't being selfish or self-centered.

Chapter 1

Simply, they were asking for what they felt belonged to them and they thought they were within their rights. Somehow Moses could read their minds. He could feel their concern for him and he knew deep down that their request was not out of selfishness or from being self-centered. Although he knew this truth, he still could not keep the anger and frustration from boiling up in his blood again.

One of the last times he was truly this furious was when he returned from Mount Sinai with the Ten Commandments and the Israelites had built false idols and were worshipping a foreign god. He remembered how he had become so furious that he lost all control, "blowing his top." In this spacious tent he thought he would lose it again. Not for the same reason as he did when he returned from Mount Sinai, but for something quite different. His blood threatened to boil in his body again because of this profound word called "investment." Moses had invested all of his time, energy, and purpose into God's people, and there were times when he wondered what his life would have been like if he had stayed in Pharaoh's palace and played by the rules. Maybe by now he would be governor over a large part of the kingdom. He would be commanding generals, armies, and territories. These thoughts did not pass through his mind often, but every once in a while they would, especially in times of difficulty and conflict. These thoughts teased him about how much he had given up, compared with how much he had ended up with as a result of answering God's call. Moses had invested so much so that God's people could be free. He invested his own future in the future of God's people and traded royalty for a life in the dusty desert for

14

years, traveling in circles hoping to reach the place of promise. He was leading people, but not generals, armies, and territories. He was leading complainers, "ungratefuls," and people who often did not see God's plan for their lives, people who talked more about returning to bondage than moving forward into prosperity. Oftentimes, the difficulty of leading people is taking them to places they can't see and managing their complaints along the way. Leaders are uniquely gifted and developed over time to withstand tension and pressure that would cause most people to buckle and bend. For years Moses dealt with the "ungratefuls," and this latest scenario was just another moment of leadership development and growth for Moses.

Do you have any "ungratefuls" in your life right now? Whenever I reconsider my call and purpose, it is typically when I feel as though I am surrounded by ungratefuls. Not to say that I am super special, but you want to feel appreciated. I think, Wow. I could be doing something else, making a lot more money, with less pressure and more respect. Ultimately these feelings eventually pass and I return to focusing less on the ungratefuls in my life and more on being grateful for the path of my life.

Moses's composure changed not because he was feeling ill, but because he was angry again. Mean words began to form and rise from the heated blood in his veins. He was older, but he still had fire. As these words reached his mind, he became frightened, realizing what he was about to say out loud. Never was there so great a challenge to hold his peace and push back his words. With

15

every ounce of energy in his body, he had to force the words back into his boiling blood, not allowing them to flow from his lips.

Moses seemed to struggle for hours with his own inner conflict, but it wasn't hours. It was moments, even seconds. The tribal leaders were still looking at him, waiting on his response, when a bright beam of light cascaded across the top of the tent. This light was not that of the setting sun; it moved quickly, much faster than the sun. This light filled the space with energy, hope, and most of all, peace. Suddenly, Moses's blood cooled and his composure reset. He didn't have to force down bad words and thoughts. He could think more clearly, and his thoughts were blended with waves of hope and love. He realized in that moment that his promised land was not their promised land.

Do you remember the moment when you realized your promise was not their promise? How did you feel? How did you handle the "news flash"? During part of my vocational journey, I had the opportunity to serve as a youth pastor. It was one of the best experiences in ministry I ever had and certainly one of the most rewarding. Youth pastors get the wonderful privilege of speaking into the lives of young people and helping them discern their future. I remember seeing young people matriculate through high school and seeing their parents hold out hope for a particular future for their students. In some cases a parent's promise aligned with his or her student's promise, but in other cases it did not. When the connection failed, these were always painful moments that left the parent feeling sad and the student affirming his or her need to live his or her own life. Maybe you have experienced moments like these in leadership when you had certain hopes and dreams for others but their reality was not tracking to your promise. Whenever this occurs, like Moses, we have to be willing to examine our true purpose and motivation.

Moses knew that he'd accomplished God's special purpose for him and completed God's call to set God's people free. He had fulfilled God's promise and the journey to the promised land for all of the people because the promised land was actually a hope and not only a place. He knew that he'd done his job, even with so many of the Israelites who never made it to the land that flowed with milk and honey. Secretly, as Moses aged year after year, he wondered if he, too, would make it to that land. He had started this journey when he was eighty years old and his brother Aaron, eighty-three. Many years had passed since that fateful day at a mesmerizing bush of fire that refused to be consumed. Whatever the light was or represented this day, it filled him with peace and a renewed purpose. Moses felt an assurance accompanied by a deeper understanding of human nature. After many years of leading people and making his own mistakes, he could see life in the panoramic portrait of God's design and realized that no journey is perfect, while all journeys are possible. Perhaps both he and the tribal leaders had been self-centered. Moses's self-centeredness could have been because he thought so highly of his personal investment in their futures. The tribal leaders' self-centeredness could have been because they focused on their own needs more than the needs of the entire Israelite community. In the presence of the light, Moses and the tribal leaders forgave one another for any offense that they caused one another, and they all knew there was hope in the space.

Chapter 1

---

*List the times when you were self-centered as a leader.
What caused you to shift away from being self-
centered to being people centered?*

Moses chuckled under his breath as he thought that for many
years he had worked so hard to make sure everyone made it to
the promised land. He never figured some of the tribes would
voluntarily make the decision to stay where they were before they
walked into God's greatest blessings. To move forward in his own
mind and spirit, he had to separate the promise from the people.
Moses had always viewed the Israelites as a promise and not a
people. He forgot they had their own hopes, dreams, and visions
for the future. He forgot the leaders of the tribes were strong and
fearless. He forgot the new generations would not have experienced slavery, the Red Sea crossing, water gushing from a dry
rock, eating manna, and being protected by a cloud by day and
fire by night. He was thinking only of their collective past and not
their individual experiences or futures. The light showed Moses
their faces in a new way. They were God's people and God had
filled each of them with a collective and individual promise of
their own. Even though he was not their father, for the first time
he felt like an aging parent looking at his grown children who
were no longer infants. They had developed their own voices and
opinions. Like any parent, it was hard to release them and trust
their decisions, but Moses had to learn how to trust and release,
even as his heart was breaking.

Leadership is a lot like parenting and consumed by trusting
and releasing. We are called to lead people through seasons and
not eternity.

Questions for Discernment

Numbers 13 describes the promised land as a place flowing
with milk and honey, pledged by God to the Israelite people, who
had been in slavery under Pharaoh in Egypt. We know that God
continues to make these kinds of promises to us today, personally
and collectively.

   1. What is your land of bondage or barrier (personally and/
      or collectively) from which you have either been delivered
      or believe God will deliver you?

   2. What is your promised land (personally and/or collec-
      tively) pledged to you by God?

Close your eyes and see the promised land that God has for
you. This land may be physical—a tangible place that you can
touch or to which you can drive or fly, a geographic location on a
map just waiting for your arrival. Or your land can be an emotion,
a passion, a dream to be happy, a desire to live without fear, or a
goal to overcome within a year. Whatever your promised land may
be—tangible or intangible—it is real. To understand God's pledge
to you is to claim it and believe that there is even more to know
and discover. No matter what your current location is, you must
keep pressing and praying until you reach your promised land.

Chapter 1

1. To where is God calling you and what is God calling you to do, even as you face disappointments along the way?

2. How do you manage the reality of your current experiences along with your knowledge of God's future promise for your life?

3. How do you handle your relationships with those who believe in you but don't support your pursuit of God's promise? Do you work to salvage your connections to them if they become strained—or not?

4. What happens when you discover that you and those with whom you're in relationship have different promises, all from God?

5. Is it possible to mature to a point at which you all can celebrate and support all of your God-given promises?

Reflection on "Beginnings" by Jacob Armstrong

Pastor, Providence Church, Mt. Juliet, TN

I remember my first day on the job as the pastor of a new church. My young family of four had moved back to my hometown to start a church for those who felt disconnected from God and the church. Having difficulty finding a place to live, we moved in with my parents for a short time. So, on my first day on the job I prepared to walk out the back door of the house in which I grew up. I was literally leaving a familiar place to go do something very unfamiliar to me. Our church had no name, no place to meet, and—oh yeah—no people. My wife, Rachel, stopped me as I turned the doorknob to begin this great journey. I will always remember the question she asked me.

"Where are you going?"

The question caught me off guard. To me, the answer seemed obvious. "I'm going to start the new church," I said. "We just uprooted our lives, believing in this dream, and I'm going to start the church."

She said, "I know. But, specifically, where are you going?"

My honest reply: "I have no idea."

Holy beginnings often include an initial step toward a land, the vision God has given us, with no idea how we will get there. We step out on faith and then step out on faith again and again and again.

As you can imagine, this means that those you journey with from time to time will cry out to the leader, "Where are we going?" It may even be more intense than that. For Moses it sounded like, "Were there not enough graves in Egypt? Did you bring us into the desert to die?" This led

Moses to ask, "Are these my children?" and say, "I can't carry this burden any longer!"

What I am getting at is, this work of leading people toward God's promise is hard. It hurts. People won't always get it. They will seem to betray you and at times actually betray you.

In the midst of reading, I would remind you to remember the beginning. Remember your initial call and the dream God gave you. Remember the stirring in your heart and the way it felt. What I learned from walking out the back door of my boyhood home is that there is no step taken that God doesn't take with you. Even and especially when you don't know where you are going, God goes with you. Don't give up. It is worth it.

Chapter 2

DIFFICULT CONVERSATIONS

As Moses led the people toward the promised land, they took a journey that was filled with many experiences, some expected and some unexpected. I don't believe Moses planned for the abrupt exit of two of the tribes along the way, and nothing could have prepared him for this lesson in leadership of having difficult conversations. Life is a journey that will take us to places we never imagined. As we know from the eternal wisdom of others, life will also keep you in those places longer than you wish to stay. These places, however, can be thrilling while they are also sometimes frightening.

In my own life, the journey has been fascinating as I have pursued my own promises, somehow and some way daring into the uncharted waters and unexplored territories of my soul and of the world around me. As I remember my days of youth, I see that God has always challenged me to step out into the unknown to a place of discomfort. Along the way I hoped for mile markers and signs to point the way to the right place and to the right person. At times the markers were people and at other times the markers seemed to be the actual voice of God directing me. These moments are the unique and special times that I needed in the most difficult days of my life, moments when the journey was long and dark and when I felt I was traveling alone. Not to compare my journey to Moses's or other biblical characters', but I believe I know what the pursuit of promise may cost and why so many people never try. All my life I have been blessed to know dreamers, and in knowing dreamers, I've come to realize there are very few who break the glass ceiling between their dreams and accomplishing their dreams. For some, they get stuck and never move into the greater possibility. I am grateful for the mile markers that reminded me that I have been in dream stage too long and need to transition to the reality of achieving my dreams no matter the cost. When I was blessed to be appointed to plant Impact Church, I had permission to dream, and with that permission came tremendous isolation and fear. Imagine floating in the ocean, far from land, and wondering if the currents would be strong enough to deliver you to your destination. I quickly realized that I could not make it on my own and that the journey would not be easy and filled with lonely moments. I rediscovered a presence within me that some would call the Holy Spirit, and I reaffirmed the promise of Matthew 28 that God would never leave me. When we feel alone, we have to remind ourselves that we are truly never alone.

In times when you feel alone, recall the promises of God. Pray that God will send you angels and mile markers to remind you along the way that you are enough and loved by the eternal Creator.

Although Moses was a gifted leader, I suspect he always struggled with difficult conversations, and that struggle continued into his years as the Israelites' leader. Back in Exodus 4:10 when Moses confessed to God that he had a stuttering problem, maybe this confession was a cover for the part of him that was afraid to speak to Pharaoh—and to God's people. Really, how easy was it to walk up to Pharaoh and say, "Hello, my name is Moses, and God sent me to tell you that you are wrong"? Talk about how leadership is filled with series of difficult conversations! Difficult conversations are inevitable along the way. Personally, I have tried to avoid difficult conversations and secretly admire people who are able to lead them with ease. As a leader I realized that there was a high frequency of need to have difficult conversations for any number of reasons. Some reasons were staff concerns, volunteer systems, ordering equipment, or lack of morale. The subjects of difficult conversations were truly all over the map and I was frustrated and furious. Not with the need to have the conversations but with my unwillingness and lack of courage in leading difficult conversations. I finally understood that I had to become stronger as a leader, develop better communication skills, and learn to open my mouth and speak to my pharaohs. Truly Moses could not have been exempt from knowing this reality, facing these types of discussions over and over again. So, when the two tribes approached him, he knew it was time for yet another challenging exchange. Yes, another conversation with Pharaoh.

Have you ever wished that those who loved you and cared for you the most would have told you that life at its best is filled with series of difficult conversations that actually lead to even more difficult conversations. Or, maybe they did tell you, or try to, but you just didn't listen. I remember reading how Jethro helped Moses understand that he could not avoid tough interactions with others.

> But you should also look among all the people for capable persons who respect God. They should be trustworthy and not corrupt. Set these persons over the people as officers of groups of thousands, hundreds, fifties, and tens. Let them sit as judges for the people at all times. They should bring every major dispute to you, but they should decide all of the minor cases themselves. This will be much easier for you, and they will share your load. (Exod 18:21-22)

Wow! This advice is profoundly wise, guiding Moses to how he should delegate power and authority. However, hidden in this wisdom is a sharp reality: "They should bring every major dispute to you." In plain print, there it is—*difficult conversations.* Jethro helped Moses understand that although others could represent him in the small cases, he still had the ultimate responsibility to handle the more complex ones. Leaders who avoid or try to delegate difficult conversations will never reach their fullest potential. They will keep the organizations they lead from reaching their greatest capacity as well. They will also stunt the growth of those who report to them or are directly connected to them in the org chart relationship. I know that you are stepping away from this thought and thinking, *I serve as a leader in a volunteer-based organization, and he is referring to for-profit organizations.* If you are thinking this, you are far from base and need to come back to reality. It is even more important to have difficult conversations in volunteer-based organizations. In the end, we can't avoid these type of conversations.

In most cases, these difficult conversations come in three categories:

1. Conversations with self
2. Conversations with others
3. Conversations with God

When my family (wife and daughter, then a one-year-old) was preparing in the summer of 2006 to plant our new church, Impact, I was plagued with so much doubt and fear that I am almost ashamed to share this very personal experience. I felt like so many other leaders who, like Moses, stood in the middle of their wilderness, hearing God's distinctive voice calling them to a wonderful plan beyond anything they could ever imagine. Although I clearly could hear God's direction for my life, I could also hear my fears, failures, and faults. To be honest, sometimes these critical voices were louder than that of God. Have you ever had moments when the noise was louder than God's voice and direction in your life? More and more I believe the real challenge of leadership is being able to clear the surround-sound noise and focus on the truth and the God choice. Most people hear the God choice, but they also hear many other choices. Sometimes young people get off track, and older adults as well, because they aren't able to concentrate only on God's voice. Over the years I have been able to clarify the noise from the real voice, but there are times when this isn't easy. When the time came to plant Impact, I was stuck and panicking and wasn't 100 percent sure that I was hearing God's voice and not my own voice or the voices of those who were helping to guide my next decision.

It was also difficult because starting a new church meant I would be leaving a wonderful position as an associate pastor at a dynamic church. Beginning this ministry meant I would be risking our family's livelihood on something I felt God was calling me to do—yet could fail. My wife, Farrah, and I had been married fewer than five years. We had a young child who was not yet three years old, and it felt as though my vision was no more than folly as I believed God for something outrageous. I remember one night, while driving on an Atlanta highway, calling Farrah with tear-filled eyes and saying, "I must plant this new church." I was finally able to express with her my dream with absolute belief because I had already had the difficult conversation with myself. I had become settled in my spirit that I was making not only the right move, but the God-move. You can tell when you meet leaders who haven't had the difficult "self" conversations. More than looking for receiving the customary encouragement and instructions, they constantly seek people to assure and reassure them of "next and now."

After you conquer difficult conversations with self, then you must conquer having difficult conversations with other people. These discussions always come with the most dynamic and interesting circumstances. In most cases as a leader, I have found these conversations revolve around vision alignment and expectations. Perhaps with me being a person whose job description is heavily weighted toward talking publicly, you may think that I would be also gifted in talking one-on-one and with small groups. I actually bomb in these two areas because no matter how much I rehearse the words and phrases in my head, they never seem to come out right. I feel embarrassed when I mix up my words. Like Moses, "I can't talk" or "I am afraid to talk." I have found that the best solution in these situations is to be honest with myself and with the person(s) to whom I'm talking. I start the conversation with my concerns, fears, and doubts. These confessions tend to release some of the tension in the atmosphere (at least for me) and allow the real words and phrases that I want to speak to flow. Here's how the beginning of such a difficult conversation may sound:

> Thank you for meeting with me today. I want to start by saying that this is a challenging discussion for me to have with you. I appreciate and value you so much that I am willing to overcome my fears for this needed discussion. Thank you for listening to me, and I promise to listen to you.

There it is. Easy? Well, maybe not so much, but I believe that if I can do it, so can you. Now it's time for you to practice.

List three people you need to have difficult conversations with. List the subject, preferred location for the conversation, desired outcome, and date to have the conversation. Now that you have completed this task, pray and ask God to give you strength to go for it and have the difficult conversation.

Finally, my conversations with God over the years have been phenomenal, but not always easy. Some people believe they can hear God's audible voice, and some believe that we only "hear"

God through nature and through the wisdom of others. I believe we can hear God speaking in whatever form is necessary for us to receive and understand. Throughout my life, I have been blessed to hear God's voice in multiple ways, even including God's audible voice. My struggles have not been regarding hearing God, but actually doing what God was telling me to do or going where God was telling me to go. Like Moses, I have used every excuse in the world as I have met God at my numerous burning bushes. However, no matter my excuse(s), God always offered a solution. These challenging interactions with God have helped to create my spirituality and soul's formation. Today, I am better and wiser because of these difficult conversations that I've had over the years with myself, others, and God.

Border Conversations

When the two leaders asked Moses for permission to leave and claim their own promise, they weren't far from moving into the promised land. Some would say that they were on the border of the promised land. Sometimes the closer you are to your promise, the more you can expect to have these kinds of confrontations, which I call "border conversations." Bruce Wilkinson, in his book *The Dream Giver*, refers to the antagonists in these conversations as border bullies.[1] I prefer to call them "border negotiators." These arbitrations occur when leaders have the hardest time managing growth within themselves and progress in relation to vision. What most leaders can't understand is why some people would rather turn around and stay where they are when they are closer to their destinations than they are to their places of departure. Leaders have an ability to keep the maps in their heads at all times of the journey. For the leader, the destination is always right around the corner. Yet for the people following the leader, the nagging question is, "Are we there yet?" These internal moments in the minds and spirits of those following create some interesting conversations.

As we get older, we are more self-aware to a certain degree, beginning to learn the depth of our own personalities. Over the years, I have reaffirmed that my default personality is one of an introvert and I don't deal well with direct conflict or confrontation. That being said, you can imagine how difficult it is for me to process border negotiations when on the inside I feel like hiding and rescheduling the conversation to a later date. This story of Moses talking to leaders headed the opposite direction physically and psychologically teaches us that in leadership we have to call on a side of us that may not be our natural default and muster up the strength and courage to have the difficult border negotiations whenever necessary. I am not saying Moses would have been like me and avoided this conflict, but if Moses was anything like his past, chances are this border conversation was not too easy. I admire people who can openly address conflict or concern wherever and whenever necessary. Of course, we know people who are too confrontational, but from those who are able to balance confrontation and negotiation wisely, we can learn great life lessons. One lesson is that leaders have to lead, and the journey is not always peaceful or without internal opposition. The most frightening part of complex border negotiations is that the entire mission can be compromised or shifted if courage isn't present. I didn't fully realize the power of dreams coming true as it relates to God's vision for our lives. When we were planting Impact, our core team of twenty-five people dreamed big dreams, but we didn't stop along the way to contemplate what would happen if those dreams came true. So in case you are wondering what happens when dreams come true, the fulfillment of our dreams naturally creates collateral damage. This damage is unavoidable, and people with the greatest intentions cannot avoid collateral damage. For instance, a wonderful volunteer agrees to help launch a new ministry effort and the launch is successful, but you quickly realize the volunteer leader is a starter and not the person who can take the ministry to the next level. A decision/negotiation has to take place, and the end result will likely be hurt feelings on behalf of the volunteer and a knot in the stomach of the leader who has to have the difficult conversation. It never fails; collateral damage is unavoidable.

A second lesson is gained from a quote by Dr. Sam Chand in his book *Leadership Pain*: "You'll grow only to the threshold of your pain."[2] When I read this quote it floored me, and when I heard Dr. Chand say it out loud in a teaching forum I had to hold back my tears. Pain is familiar to every leader, and pain was persistent in Moses's journey as well. In most cases when you see leaders plateau and cease to reinvent themselves, that is when they have secretly or publicly said, "No more pain." Let's be clear: the pain Dr. Chand is referring to is not self-inflicted and abusive pain but the pain all leaders face when they are forced to make the tough decisions. Remember: lesson one is all about collateral damage and lesson two is all about pain management. You probably have never heard the phrase *pain management* outside of the medical community, but it is near and dear to the leadership community. Would you believe me if I told you that leadership has a lot to do with pain management? Every difficult conversation that involves confrontation causes pain, and whenever you decide you've had enough pain, you plateau and so does the organization you are leading. We often justify decline by saying customers don't like the product or parishioners are just too busy to come to worship. These are all window-dressing excuses for the real truth that you became tired of negotiating the pain of leadership and surrendered to a pain-free life and existence.

If these two lessons hit home, know that you are not alone and I personally have to be taught both of them time after time and never seem to get it on the first pass. Over the years I have invested time and money in coaching opportunities to help advance my leadership to the next level. Although this resource is not about coaching, it is about receiving the help we need to confront the tough decisions we will all face in life. In each of my coaching sessions, I have always been reminded of my role as a leader and the power I have to confront the elephant in the room or avoid the elephant in the room. The choice is my choice and the choice is your choice. I hope your leadership style releases you into an arena where you feel more comfortable with positive confrontation and don't get lost in the painful abyss of mediocrity always passing the buck or hoping things will get better over time.

Our natural tendency is to freeze or stall during these difficult conversations. The freeze and stall prolongs the time to solve the real issues facing us. The elephant in the room doesn't go away because we are afraid to face it. The elephant actually gets bigger. Moses faced his elephants, and we face our elephants as well. Elephants don't just disappear; they only go away through negotiation and confrontation. So, as you are reading this section, you know about a situation in your life that is current and real. You are aware of it because it causes you the most leadership pain at the moment and is with you as the first thought in the morning and the last thought at night. You have made every excuse to pray it away and hope it away, but it won't seem to go away. Here is the truth: it won't go away until you negotiate it away or confront it away. Take the time today to develop a strategy of negotiation and confrontation. Develop your strategy to overcome your elephant right now, and don't put it off another second.

In the story, the two leaders went to Moses in private, beginning their conversation with small talk and ending with a painful request. Let's listen to their conversation again: "Moses, it seems like it was just yesterday that we were in bondage in Egypt. There was no hope of a future, and God sent you. We are so grateful for all you have done for us and all you continue to do. This is why it is so difficult to ask, 'Moses, may we leave the journey?'"

Although they asked to leave, they were really asking permission to stay where they were. This concept is what some psychologists would call a paradox. Overtly and publicly they were asking to leave, but subconsciously their desire was to stay where they were. Specifically and geographically, where were they? Historians have said they were in the Transjordan, "a relatively high plateau cut across by numerous wadis. Four major wadis divide the region: the Wadi Yarmuk which enters the Jordan just south of Galilee, the River Jabbok just over halfway between Galilee and the Dead Sea, the River Arnon which enters the Dead Sea about halfway down the east side, and the Brook Zered which enters the Dead Sea at its southern end."[3] As you can see, they were in an area of prime real estate where resources were abundant. No wonder these tribes wanted to remain in this place. If I had been traveling through the wilderness for years and suddenly entered a space along the journey that was fertile and prosperous, I would likely have reconsidered my commitment of traveling to the promised land as well. Even when we don't admit it, there is always a little ounce of risk in trusting promises even if they are promises from God. These tribes were risking everything, and as they risked everything they had to constantly ask themselves if it was worth it and if it was in their best interest to move forward.

This is why vision and leadership go hand in hand, because leaders like Moses are constantly painting new pictures to a place in front of people to show the way and to encourage them along the way. This is why Kirbyjon Caldwell described the vision process for leaders in the following way:

> One way a true Vision can be recognized is that everyone around you will not agree with it. By definition, a Vision stretches reality; it's not a quick and easy fix. It's a mountain that rises up in your line of sight, at first foreboding, seemingly impossible. But the closer you get, the more attainable it becomes—if you can persevere in the face of the negative forces that are going to rise up against you.[4]

The Reubenites and the Gadites only saw their current location, which was the Transjordan, but they could not see their future location: Canaan, the land flowing with milk and honey.

Now you see why this moment was a defining one in Moses's leadership: because he had to negotiate the possibility of releasing the hope and desire he had for all of the Israelites by allowing some of them to dream and hope for themselves. It is difficult to embrace the idea of people choosing their own paths, especially when we feel they are choosing the status quo and not the bright hope of the future. This particular instance for Moses was filled with a deep and passionate pause as he thought through the depth of the negotiation. In life and especially in leadership, there are many important periods filled with grand pauses. These pauses are lived out like an unchoreographed dance routine. These pauses can make or break us. They are defining moments in our leadership. Remember, don't freeze or stall. It is only a pause, and you will make it to the next level and phase.

Are you experiencing a pause moment right now in your life, ministry, or organization? How does it feel? Is it debilitating or inspiring? Through prayer, reflection, and courage, transform your pause moment into an opportunity moment.

Sad to say, some people get trapped in the pause and never find their way out of their internal mazes. They get lost in the fear, decision, and responsibility or challenge that awaits them on the other side of the pause. Perhaps for a second, Moses wanted to give up or withdraw in the midst of the pause. Maybe he thought for a moment, like the other two leaders, that their current location was far enough or good enough. Maybe he secretly wondered in the pause if he had what it took to lead the people into their future. Maybe for one moment in the pause he was relieved by their request because he had been thinking the same thing and didn't have the courage to utter the words. Here he was in the middle of nowhere facing the pause of his life. Some would say it was a midlife crisis, but Moses was well beyond the middle of his life. Truly he'd seen enough sunsets and glowing stars in the sky to know that life could never turn out as expected or desired. All eyes were on Moses; he was the leader.

Who is currently journeying with you and deep down you know they are asking "May I leave?" Are your insecurities as a leader keeping them in a place that no longer fits their purpose or God's plan?

"May I leave?" requests are never easy. As a matter of fact, they are painful and frightening at the same time. There are two types of "leave" requests. The first is when someone leaves by choice. This type is much like the scene with Moses and the two tribes. The tribes made a choice and requested to leave. Leaving by choice would seem to be the easier of the two types, but often it is not. Those who have cared for young persons as a parent, grandparent, foster parent, or guardian know what I mean. To hear the young person one day utter the question, "May I leave?" is quite difficult. We mentally understand the request, but for some reason our emotions never seem to catch up with what we know or understand; herein lies the rub. How do we offer a rational answer with our emotional feelings? This reconciliation of experiences

37

is hard because we have been wired to think that if they leave, we lose rather than gain. We lose a companion, a child, a responsibility, a friend, a resource, a place, or a space. If they leave, then we begin to wonder, "What if everyone else or everything else decides to leave too?" I imagine the pause for Moses took so long because he was facing a leadership crisis that we all face at our jobs, at home, and at play. We somehow take a huge thought leap and believe if one group leaves, then everyone will leave us; and if we are not careful, we can spend wasted time in a place and space that is unhappy, making shameless bargains and deals to keep temporary people in our lives who were never supposed to have a permanent designation on our journey. Although we may forever be connected, the type and frequency of connection may change over time. So now here is the hard choice, and I can't help you outside of encouraging you to take the opportunity the next time someone asks, "May I leave?" and offer the following answer: "Yes, and I pray God's grace and favor over your life."

The second "May I leave?" request is not by choice, but by mandate. I know the word *mandate* is difficult for people to hear because so many of us retreat from mandatory requirements out of fear of being told what to do and how to behave. I remember as a child wanting to grow up so that I would no longer have to do what my mother instructed—things like making up my bed, helping to wash clothes, and having to be at home by a certain time. Now that I am older, I realize that I cannot escape all mandatory requirements. As an adult, I feel I actually have fewer freedoms than I had as a child. These mandatory leave moments can be hard because we don't have a choice, and in a world that is excited about choices, we are faced with moments when we have to live with the decisions others have made that impact our lives. We all wish that those who are with us and aren't deeply committed would come to us and say, "I have to leave." Rarely is this the case, and most times it is the deeply committed person or couple that says, "It's time to leave." I have had many occasions where individuals were called away because of work and life and had no choice and left.

When is the last time someone left physically, spiritually, and emotionally because of mandatory reasons? Remember: people are always leaving for one reason or another, and it is important that we keep it in perspective.

I think this pause was so long because Moses knew that this mandatory leave request would affect all of the Israelites. Their decision was so dynamic that the biblical recorders felt it was necessary to record it in the sacred scrolls of the Hebrew Bible. So significant was Moses's response to their request that it would make or break the next phase of his leadership. These are the particular instances that place knots of anxiety in your stomach, keep you up late at night, and awaken you early in the morning without the assistance of an alarm. These pauses are the kind we will never forget. Remember: these pauses during difficult conversations always lead to "Goodbye."

Goodbye

During the difficult conversations, we are faced with one of the most powerful words in history: "goodbye." It is ironic that this word begins with "good." How can a departure be good? Moses looked at the two tribal leaders with tear-filled eyes and a scratchy throat and said, "Goodbye." In all the years of his leadership, this was one of the most trying farewells for him despite it being a simple combination of two words, *good* and *bye*. The more he thought about these words individually, the more conflicted he became on the inside. How can a "bye" be good? He remembered the times of separation in his life and recalled that they were never good or easy. The day when his mother bid goodbye to him as he floated down the Nile River, under the watchful eyes of his sister. The abrupt goodbye he uttered to those who helped raise him after he committed the awful crime of murder. The farewell he whispered to Jethro as he answered God's call and launched out to lead God's people. Each of these goodbyes helped to prepare him for one of the most difficult "goodbye" moments in his life. As a leader he had officiated over many disputes, decisions, and deaths. He thought his skin was tough and his emotions were strong, but for some reason, this goodbye was not good, but difficult.

Although he felt awful on the inside, he wished them well and entreated God's favor over them. Neither leaving nor being left is ever easy. Moving on means we either have to say goodbye or are forced to hear goodbye. Parting ways happens all throughout our lives. When children visit their noncustodial parent for a couple of weeks during a school break, many develop a deep ache as the time to return home draws near, dreading the need to articulate goodbye. After a high school romance carries over into summer, the couple utters goodbye as they depart for separate colleges. Holding your sister's weary hands at her bedside while whispering a final farewell, witnessing how an illness has robbed her body of vitality, becomes the most agonizing "goodbye" of your life. We fight to hold back tears and anger when we sit in a room with our manager, hearing that the company we gave twenty years to no longer needs our contribution and has asked us to leave the premises by the end of the day. If we are lucky, we are allowed to send a final e-mail to our coworkers: "I am moving on. I wish each of you well. Goodbye."

So you are at the top of the world and your game and suddenly you hear the whisper "Goodbye." How did you handle this new reality, or did this new reality handle you?

One of the stories above is particularly personal for me. As a boy I visited my dad for the summer. As each summer break with my dad came to an end, it was difficult to say goodbye. This might be why I still struggle with it today as an adult in a vocation where departures can happen every single day due to multiple types of circumstances. I can remember walking down the airplane tunnel to board the plane, still feeling my father's embrace as tears formed in the corners of my eyes. I struggled to look back, wave with a smile, and say, "Goodbye, Daddy."

Moses must have felt these kinds of accompanying feelings as he said his farewells. These were members of his leadership team. These were tribal members he had cared for and nurtured along the way. Goodbyes are never easy, and the more I think about it, the more I believe they aren't supposed to be comfortable. If they were painless, that would mean that we didn't care that much about the places, or the person, or the moments we spent there or with them.

41

I can also recall times in my life when I so disliked a person or a situation that I practiced and rehearsed my goodbye. I couldn't wait to leave, wait to be free, wait to do my own thing and live my own life. I practiced and rehearsed my farewell speech. Leaving under those circumstances was rather easy, but there comes a time in our lives when it isn't so effortless anymore. Parting ways is painful. To nurture is to love and to love is to hold close. Goodbyes can cause us to learn how to love and nurture from a distance. These leaders would never forget Moses's love and nurturing spirit. He helped raise and shape their worldviews. Through Moses they grew in wisdom and leadership. Both Moses and these leaders would have to learn how to love and nurture from a distance. They would have to accept that a "goodbye" can always be right around the corner and that saying so will never be easy.

Questions for Discernment

In life, there are many goodbye moments that are difficult to experience, especially when we are on the receiving end of them. These moments can even be disguised as requests such as, "May I stay?"

1. How do you handle the goodbye moments in your life? Is the experience different according to whether you were on the receiving or giving end of the goodbye? What are the differences?

2. Has anyone ever disguised a goodbye as a request to you? How did you feel when you realized where this difficult conversation was actually headed?

3. Generally, how do you handle difficult conversations? How has what you've learned on this promised land journey influenced or changed how you handle difficult conversations?

**Reflection on "Difficult Conversations"
by Rodney Thomas Smothers**

**Lead Pastor, Liberty Grove UMC,
Burtonsville, MD**

"Difficult Conversations" is a journey through the twist and turns of exploration, self-examination, and excavation of a leader's cycle of call, chaos, and comfort. The biblical story of Moses's challenge to lead while his position of leadership was being questioned is a place in which every leader has found him- or herself. This story provides us with a bird's-eye view of the inner conversations that every courageous leader has experienced.

Balancing the "go" mandate of God while navigating the doubts of followers takes not only skill but inner strength. This special type of anointed leadership requires a constant recalibrating of the purpose and plans when we are faced with an ever-changing landscape accompanied by fickle and fearful followers. We experience in this story the three stages of difficult conversations: with ourselves, with others, and with God. Masterfully woven into the tapestry of doubt and decision, fear and faith, rebellion and reward, this chapter lets us overhear how these inner voices are tamed.

These difficult conversations are indeed anchored in the alignment of vision and expectations, knowing that what we heard from God can be trusted to lead us to God's intended victory. The naming of these places of decisions as "border conversation" renews in us an awareness that all great efforts come with criticism from those who can't see what we as leaders see. In spite of the detours, we are reminded not to allow the mission to be compromised.

Preventing our God-given dreams from being side-tracked when others are requesting permission to abandon the journey is a double-edged leadership sword. Do I remind them of the promise and insist that they continue with me, or do I allow their fear to cause them to be left behind? Courageous leadership weighs those goodbye moments as difficult conversations, but sometimes those conversations lead to painful necessary endings.

Departures and destiny both require the type of deep introspection that is rooted in a clear picture of God's preferred future. While the discussions can be difficult, the destination can never be in doubt. This chapter provides us with a set of proven skills to navigate to God's intended victory.

YOUR PROMISE, MY CHOICE

The Reubenites and Gadites were part of a larger group of tribes whose history began with Abraham receiving a promise from God that his descendants would number the stars and the sand on the beaches. God's word was true, and Abraham's family stretched throughout the earth and became the twelve tribes of Israel. The Reubenites and Gadites were part of the twelve tribes along with Simeon, Judah, Issachar, Zebulun, Benjamin, Dan, Naphtali, Asher, Ephraim, and Manasseh. The Reubenites and Gadites weren't the largest, most powerful, or most influential of the tribes, but their role was significant as a part of the twelve, and their presence was important to Moses and to all of the other tribes. The tribe of Reuben found its place in history as the descendent from Reuben who was the firstborn son to Jacob and Leah. The tribe of the Gadites descended from Jacob's seventh son, born to Zilpah.

The potential impact of their absence was probably much like that experienced by younger children when an older sibling leaves for college or to serve in the military. Some may meander through the house, feeling the empty rooms and space. Others may be overjoyed that the house suddenly became less crowded. The rest may not feel one way or the other. No matter the experience of those "left behind," they get used to feeling the void.

For the tribes who felt indifferently about the Reubenites and the Gadites departing, when they received the news, they thought, *Here they go again! Always trying to leave and go their separate ways and do their own thing. They always come back. It's only a temporary excursion.* However, this request to Moses was different, and the other tribes came to know that they were definitely leaving. Decisions to separate are never easy for the one making them or the ones being impacted by the occurrence. These tribes had traveled together all of their lives, and they didn't know any other people. So, having two of their own leave was likely not only devastating but also an awakening experience. Moses and the elders could not help but wonder if the other tribes would be influenced by the Reubenites and Gadites. Would they also catch a case of wanderlust and make a similar decision to part ways early, to abort the entire Israelite community's mission of reaching the land of promise? Wondering if other tribes would decide to follow a path similar to the tribes of Reuben and Gad was quite a quandary for Moses. Internal concern grew daily among the elders. Realizing that God had given Moses a promise that was not necessarily that of each tribe was more of a dilemma for Moses than anything else. The Reubenites and Gadites actually had a choice to follow the larger plan—or not.

"Wanderlust" is the potential for people to dream about what can be even when they are in the midst of something that seems awesome to the outside world.

> *Therefore it is difficult for the dreamer to explain*
> *to the nondreamer the depth of what he or she sees.*
> *Sometimes wanderlust is so powerful it causes us to*
> *say goodbye.*

Yes. Leadership is all about showing people the future while knowing deep down that they may not choose the future we see for them. This reality is painful to face. Teachers face this dilemma in the classroom as they begin the school year, seeing their students who are filled to the brim with potential. Yet they know in their hearts how all of that potential can be compromised by the outside forces in their homes, communities, peers—and even by their own internal forces and decisions. All teachers want only the best for their students, consciously and unconsciously setting high hopes and expectations for them while fearing the possibility of a future day of dashed hopes and disappointment because a student chooses a different path. Sometimes teachers may even feel the choice is that of a lesser path. In Andy Stanley's work *Next Generation Leader,* he concludes, "Leaders provide a mental picture of a preferred future and then ask people to follow them there."[1] I agree with Stanley's belief on leadership, but I believe he would also agree that from time to time people won't follow even when the picture is painted in the highest and clearest pixel rating of the culture.

No one will ever know if Moses felt that the path the Reubenites and the Gadites took was a lesser one, but it was surely not the path of promise God had given to the Israelites through Moses. Definitely, though, these two tribes were not electing to go to a land that flowed with milk and honey. Moses had to come to grips with this different path as their choice, their decision. It brings to remembrance the final stanza of Robert Frost's renowned poem "The Road Not Taken":

> I shall be telling this with a sigh
> Somewhere ages and ages hence:
> Two roads diverged in a wood, and I—
> I took the one less traveled by,
> And that has made all the difference.[2]

As leaders we are constantly engaging our internal compass to determine the right road or path to take. Although we are responsible for others, we must be sure we are personally taking the right path. It was important for Moses to stay on course no matter the cost. Often in my leadership journey, I am constantly juggling the wishes of people and the vision God has given me to follow. I wish I could honestly say God wins each time, but I can't. Sometimes people and their agendas win and I take a different path. I am glad that Moses didn't lose his way but kept the path God had chosen for his life and the Israelites. I am also glad Moses's leadership capacity was big enough to allow the Reubenites and Gadites to choose their own path even if it wasn't the path he would have chosen. Only time and destiny can reveal if it was Moses or the Reubenites and Gadites who took the road less traveled. On your journey you will face this road over and over again, and sometimes you will go God's way and sometimes you will go your way, but in either case you will be on your way. Keep moving and never stop, and eventually, like Moses, the Reubenites, and the Gadites, you will find your road and it will be the "road less traveled."

It is true we have been talking about the decisions and the roads traveled by the Reubenites, the Gadites, and Moses for "ages and ages."

All leaders before Moses and after have discovered that although the promises God gave them were real, God also gave other promises to those who were following them. When people exercise their will to select their own promises, their choices don't always mean that they disagree with our path. Rather it simply means that they have their own passions, dreams, and destiny that demand they go another way. Perhaps, even, it was Moses's passion for his promise that inspired the Reubenites and the Gadites to live their own promise. Sometimes our passionate commitments to our personal promise ignites a fire within someone else to live his or her own promise. Eventually, we have to make a choice to live someone else's promise or our own promise.

Once, when I was making a big life decision, I sought the wisdom of a spiritual mentor. Since I had never opened myself to this opportunity before, I did not know what to expect. Well, that's not true. I did expect to see the stars, the moon, and some super-spiritual stuff happen in the room while meeting with the spiritual mentor. To my amazement, the experience was less fantastic than I thought, and to some degree it was a letdown. After I emptied my heart of all the uncertainty I was experiencing, the mentor simply told me to "make a decision." I left in awe of what I had heard, feeling empowered to know that I serve a God who gives me a choice. I understood that when I was created there wasn't a red car custom-designed for me to drive when I turned sixteen and got my driver's license. Rather, there were red, blue, green, and yellow cars that had not been designed specifically for me, but from which I was free to choose. Whichever one of these options I selected, it would be a good car for me to drive. I now know God's promises for my life are directly connected to the capacity that God has given me to choose, and my choices lead to the fulfillment of my destiny. The next step to fulfilling your destiny is up to you, and it is your choice. Remember: Moses met God at the burning bush, but he still had to make a decision to follow God's plan for his life. Certainly, we are all grateful Moses chose God's way and not his own. As you contemplate your next big choice, I hope you make the right God choice and not the choice that is best for you or your current circumstances. Moses made a choice, and the Reubenites and the Gadites made a choice. We can choose to live in the theological debate of their choice thousands of years ago or live in the reality of our today and take advantage of the opportunity to make the God choice for our lives today. The spiritual guide was right—"make a decision."

Decision Follows Request

Once we make a request to follow our own promises, everyone affected must then make a decision. Understanding this dynamic is tricky because on the surface we can say that the request of the Reubenites and Gadites was mandatory, that Moses had no choice in the matter. In our own lives and situations, we can think that we have no choice when others tell us they wish to leave. Yet, like Moses, we always have the opportunity to make a choice, one that is both strategic and spiritual. In the natural, we may think that Moses's decision would be an ordinary one. It was not. He had to operate on a much deeper physiological and spiritual level in this critical moment of leadership that could have altered so many future events for the Israelites. These moments of decision must not be taken lightly; they must be treated with the utmost care. Moses understood this time in their journey was a big one. What he chose to say and do could possibly cause other tribes to decide to remain where they were and not proceed to the promised land. He also knew that if he disappointed these two tribes by not meeting their request they could start a revolt among the other tribes.

Moses's role as a leader had never been easy and should have prepared him for such a critical time. However, for a moment or two he became stuck. Well, perhaps *stuck* is too strong a word. Often we do not want to assign such labels to our leaders, especially biblical ones, those whom we hold in high esteem and deem to have been perfect beings. The truth of the matter is that all leaders get stuck from time to time. I believe this happens because we don't always have a clear road map to what is next, and the road ahead can become confusing. I am grateful that Moses found a way to move forward from being stuck and pulled himself out of that dazed and perplexing situation. Maybe he recalled the wisdom of his father-in-law or that of his wife, but something awakened him to the moment, and for that I am grateful. Actually, all of us ought to give thanks for that reawakened moment. In that instant, Moses showed us the whole dynamic of living and leading. We all face tough and difficult situations, and if we are not careful, we can come to a slow halt and cease to be the people God created us to be. These halts and slow stops are hard to notice because they happen gradually over time and space. Without noticing we can find ourselves living into the pause, sitting on the side of the road watching the vehicles of destiny and purpose pass us by.

When was the last time you became stuck? How did you feel and how long were you stuck? Three keys to moving again: (1) Pray. (2) Ask for help. (3) Believe in yourself.

Standing alone with these two tribal leaders, Moses was on the edge of having to make a decision that would impact so many people. This was a big decision because it was both strategic and spiritual. Strategically, Moses was responsible for the bottom line of this movement in the Israelites' history. When we read the Bible we often don't think of it in business terms, like a return on investment (ROI) or the bottom-line narrative. Yet the reality is that God hired Moses as the CEO of God's deliverance mission for the Israelites. As such, Moses had a job to complete, delivering all of them to the promised land. The ROI for God was having an entire nation of people arrive in a safe place in order to fulfill their purpose for God's kingdom. The bottom line for Moses was a full delivery. He intended to be responsible and accountable for nothing less than that.

Although leaders are responsible for the bottom line, eventually they wake up to the reality that who started will not end with them on the journey. If I had a dollar for each time I received this lesson, I would be a millionaire. Although that money would do wonders in my bank account, it has had little comfort for my heart.

Every leader knows this reality intellectually; it is heart wrenching emotionally. Allow me to offer you the wisdom you already know: "Many people will start with you, but fewer will end with you."

Accountability as the Bottom Line

Now, there's a word for us contemporary people—*accountable*—that we don't hear much in today's society. In a conversation with a group of passionate young leaders, the word *accountable* was mentioned, which impressed me all the more. I recall one of the leaders explaining his role in the organization to which I was speaking. He told me, "I am accountable." This affirmation struck me, not because I am unfamiliar with this concept operating in the lives of young people, but because the word's meaning had taken a new shuffle on my life's playlist. Accountability is important because God sees us leaders as guardians or caretakers of resources for which we are responsible, including the people who follow our lead. Maybe this level of accountability is what makes being the one out front so challenging at times. When we lead we recognize and know things that others may want to avoid or dismiss; therefore, we remain, the ones who are accountable.

> *Name a time under your leadership when someone's decision negatively impacted an entire group. What did you do?*

Moses must have wondered how God was holding these tribal leaders responsible for not seeming to see that their leave request would affect an entire nation of people. When they approached him, they were considering only their needs and not those of their fellow Israelites. These leaders were not fully bearing in mind the promise that God had given them. God did not proclaim a pre–promised land or an almost-there place or a promised land substitute. No. God was clear about a real place, a land flowing with milk and honey. Moses had to be the one to consider more than their spoken requests; he had to factor in the unspoken needs of the rest of God's people and the promise that God had given to them through him. He was the one, as his mind quickly reviewed the precious moments with his brother, Aaron; his conversations with his father-in-law, Jethro; and of course, the moment of standing at a burning bush in the middle of a desert. He was the one facing the Israelites, convincing them with a stammering tongue, with a directive of liberation from God. He was the one facing Pharaoh, even when all the people were afraid. Moses realized he was also expecting a return on his own investment! Sometimes leadership is learning to press forward in the midst of a crowd of people who don't fully understand the promise yet want all of the benefits of the promise. In other words, they want all the benefits of the promise with no process.

Strategically Spiritual: Deal-Making at Its Best

Refusing to allow his reflections to rekindle his anger, Moses chose to recognize that these recalled moments were still close to his heart, but seemed so long ago. He had started this profound journey when he was eighty years old. To be honest, he had felt that he was a little old for the task then. Almost forty years later, his body was much older with feet that signified the many steps he had taken since God spoke to him at the burning bush. Although his body was older and his bones were becoming more and more weary, his heart and soul could still feel the passion of God's voice whenever God spoke to him. His entire life flashed in front of him in seconds, and somehow all of his many experiences seemed to have led to this very moment. From a tear of remembrance to a smile of joy, he understood what this moment was all about for him, for the Israelites. This moment was a strategic one that he had to manage as another step and test before the people were released into God's promise.

Our lives are filled with strategic decisions that we make willingly sometimes and at other times forcibly. These moments are never stress-free; they are tension-filled. In these moments, like Moses, we can think back on the days that were simpler and clearer. We could long to escape our present realities to more serene and pleasant times, but unfortunately a discreet getaway isn't possible. We all face such longings in one way or another. I encourage you to follow Moses's example and make a strategic decision to help protect the bottom line and remain accountable to God and God's people.

He counted the costs and realized it was in the best interests of everyone if the two tribes left.

However, Moses didn't stop with just granting their request. He remained a shrewd business leader; he negotiated a unique deal before releasing them. Moses said to the tribal leaders, "I will let you leave if you agree to go with us to help us fight for the land of promise. Once we receive the promise you can return to this place." The two tribal leaders tried to hold back their smiles as much as they could. With deep voices they said to Moses, "We agree and accept your offer." They hugged Moses, leaving his tent to return to their camp to share the news with their fellow leaders.

Moses's decision was strategic because the only way the land could be captured was through war, and he needed all of his soldiers on board. Today, I know war is a painful reality for those who love the Bible, tending always to see God as a God of grace and kindness. However, the road to the promised land was filled with the blood of those who already inhabited the land and filled with the blood of the Israelites who died in battles along the way. Moses needed all of those who were capable to help fight for the promise. His strategic decision was to negotiate a great deal that would accomplish their ultimate goal. Deal-making is a part of our lives, but we don't talk about it enough (out loud) in our spiritual circles.

When I was younger, I always thought things simply happened the right way if we did the right things and made sure we stuck to the right script. As I grew older and life removed the curtain of naiveté from my experiences, I started noticing certain behaviors and phenomena related to life and how things were being altered around me. I now know that I was detecting people making deals. Parents negotiate to get their children into a particular school. People promise God all kinds of sacrifices as they return to the doctor for their annual physicals, knowing that they have maintained not one of their lifestyle changes since the last doctor visit. Children make deals with loved ones for just the right holiday or birthday gift. Life at times seems to be: (1) a series of deals, and (2) living between the deals to see if the negotiations will be successful. Sometimes these arrangements are bad and sometimes they are good, but at the end of the day, they are deals.

When and what was the last deal you made? How did it turn out? Was it successful or unsuccessful? What did it cost you personally, financially, organizationally, and spiritually?

Being at Peace and Facing What's Next

Throughout his tenure as the Israelites' CEO, Moses was shrewdly strategic. He also felt the glow and passion of God's favor; therefore his decision was equally spiritual. In his day, God's voice was clear and direct to those who followed God. Moses was blessed to hear God's call and voice in his life as well as through the community of the Israelites. One could argue that if they could hear God as Moses did, they would have served God faithfully just as he did. The truth is that following God had less to do with hearing God's voice than it did with connecting with the spirit of God.

Moses's life was one of connection; we can see how his life's journey demonstrated these connections. Moses was linked to his mother and sister, who watched him float into the arms of safety down the Nile River. He was connected to Pharaoh's home and favor, even as he experienced his own internal conflicts. He was connected to the story of God's people, and his legacy will forever live through his works of faithfulness as a great deliverer. Moses was strategic and spiritual. Such a combination is a demonstration of how leaders must be equipped today so that they remain connected to God, God's people, and God's promise—while being accountable to their assignments (strategic bottom lines). Notice, although the Reubenites and the Gadites chose another promise, Moses remained connected strategically and spiritually to the promise he was given in the desert, standing beside a burning bush. So what happened? What did Moses do as a strategic and spiritual leader? He decided to protect his bottom line (strategic move) and to remain accountable to God (spiritual move).

What were the last strategic and spiritual moves you made? What was the outcome?

After the two leaders left, Moses sat in his tent alone, thinking about his deal-making, wondering if it was the right call or not. He wondered, *What if other tribes hear about my decision and make the same request? What if I've compromised too much? What if God is displeased with my decision and is angry with me? What if Jethro were alive? What would he think?* Whatever the answers to these questions were, Moses and the leaders had inked the agreement. All parties had agreed to it, and no changes could be made. Only time would determine the wisdom of Moses's negotiation. He knew it wouldn't take long for the other leaders to hear the news, to confront him to inquire about his decision and thought process. Moses knew the night would be long. He just kept breathing and telling himself, "The deal is done. I made my decision and I am at peace."

Questions for Discernment

We are called by God to be strategic and spiritual. As is life, sometimes we may feel more spiritual than strategic or more strategic than spiritual. Navigating these times is a constant balancing act, and honestly, we don't always get it right.

1. What are the strategic deals and decisions that God is impressing upon your heart as you contemplate your next?

2. Are you able to give others permission to dream and pursue those dreams, especially when this pursuit may mean leaving the commitment they made to help you reach your promised land?

3. How do you help people understand that when we choose different promises it doesn't mean that we no longer choose each other?

Reflection on "Your Promise, My Choice"
by Telley Lynnette Gadson

Senior Pastor and Spiritual Coach, Saint Mark
United Methodist Church, Taylors/Greenville, SC

When we lead, we recognize and know things that others may want to avoid or dismiss; therefore, we remain, the ones who are accountable.
—Olu Brown

"The buck stops here!" "You have to pay the cost to be the boss!" "If you can't stand the heat, get out of the kitchen!" These musings represent familiar vernacular of leadership advice. In essence, the message is conveyed that a leader, especially a leader with a desire to be effective, must take on the mantle of accountability, the helmet of responsibility, and the shield of focus (not to be confused with tunnel vision). The final analysis is the picture of a risk-taker—one who knows there are challenges, distractions, and obstacles, but he or she has seen promise in God's promises, and makes the decision to press on to the land of opportunity.

What kind of accountability, responsibility, and focus does it take to equip a congregation to step forward with a building project in the midst of an economic recession? If I had to testify, I would say that this trilogy is closely related to the kind of faith it takes to practice what is preached when God sends a gentleman with an offer to sell your church 20.6 acres of land for $75,000, but the message from the masses is, "How can we afford 'steak' when 'chicken' is causing us to rob Peter to pay Paul?"

My name is Reverend Telley Lynnette Gadson, and I am forty-two years old. I am in my seventeenth year of serving God and God's people in full-time pastoral ministry, and I am a risk-taker. In 1999, for my first appointment, I was sent to a two-point charge in Sumter, South Carolina. Fast-forward five years and that two-point charge, Mount Zion and Saint Mark United Methodist Churches, experienced a historic transition when Saint Mark became a stationed church with yours truly charged with the accountability, responsibility, and focus to serve as the church's first full-time pastor (as they would no longer share a pastor with a sister church). I was 30 years old, the church was 130 years old, and the people were looking to me to look to Jesus to lead us across the street to build on our land of promise.

But . . . how do you tell the congregation that the biggest giver has decided to leave the church because of an impasse with you, the pastor? Did I mention that three banks turned us down for financing? And . . . how do you help a faithful and trusting congregation now process the practice of the theory that the budget would increase by 50 percent almost overnight with the station move? When is it okay to challenge the status quo to live in the standard of excellence when mediocrity is often so flirtatious? On top of all that . . . how do you calm your own spirit and bless your own heart when your lows are beginning to outweigh your highs? Well . . . you remind yourself that God's calling on your life was not a suggestion, your response was not an opinion, and your way forward rests in you making the choice to trust the promises of the Promise Keeper!

Time came and time went. Unforeseen issues showed up without RSVP! We even dealt with real serpents trying to make their beds among us. Some expectations were unrealistic, and some decided the vision was too risky. As Olu Brown wrote earlier in the chapter, "These moments are never stress-free; they are tension filled."

Yet, God was absolutely faithful! On Sunday, April 9, 2010, God's blessed people walked on the promised land of 20.6 acres. We marched into a newly built edifice flowing with milk, honey, and a reasonable mortgage. We praised and worshipped the God of Moses, the twelve tribes, and the twelve disciples! We made a decision . . . the deal was done . . . and God still gets the glory!

Chapter 4

AVAILABILITY

O nce the Reubenites and Gadites left Moses's presence, he tried to take some much-needed time to rest. As he began to doze off, he sensed an instant emptiness in the air. It was the type of void we feel in our stomachs when we know that something important is missing. This emptiness seemed to linger for a long time as Moses sat alone in his tent. Although he wished for sleep, he quickly released this hope and waited for the elders to come and talk to him about the deal he made with the two tribes. Moses was a leader with great power, but in this moment he did not feel his strength or the need to use it, if he had felt forceful at all. Deep down he knew that he could have decided that the Reubenites and Gadites had to stay. He had the power and the authority to force them to stay and relinquish their seemingly childish ideas about remaining in a place outside of God's promise for them. He could have made them stay by force, but he didn't use this option. In this instance, Moses chose what Henri Nouwen called "a theology of weakness." This theology

challenges us to look at weakness not as a worldly weakness that allows us to be manipulated, . . . but as a total and unconditional dependence on God that opens us to the true channels of the divine power that heals the wounds of humanity and renews the face of

the earth. The theology of weakness claims power, God's power, the
all-transforming power of love.[1]

Moses *did* choose power, but not his own power or authority.
He chose the power of God to love and not the power of force or
hate. With this decision he reaffirmed his ability to be a great leader.
You are likely familiar with business consultant Jim Collins's coun-
sel to be a good leader versus a great leader.[2] I believe we should all
strive to be leaders who are great and seek to multiply themselves
and develop other great leaders. Allow me to offer another glimpse
into the quality of a great leader. Most people want to be leaders
and ultimately great leaders so they have the power to make significant decisions others will follow. The truth about being a great
leader is that the greater the leader you become, the fewer decisions
you will make, and your leadership style shifts from decision making to influence building. There was a time in Moses's leadership
when he had to make every decision and use the power of decision
making constantly to take a less-than-hospitable group of people
to a better place. As time moved on, Moses's power shifted from
decisions to influence, and great leaders know that true power is
not in how many decisions we can make but in how many people
we can influence. Henri Nouwen is right: we practice a theology
of weakness, not so that we are weak in our leadership but so that
we yield to the power of God and through God's power we influence people and the world. Moses used his influence and decided
not to make a decision that would have gotten in the way of the
choice made by the Reubenites and the Gadites. Although Moses knew thousands would leave who were a part of the tribes of
the Reubenites and the Gadites, he also knew he would influence

hundreds of thousands more who would remain under his leadership and travel with him to the promised land.

I have also experienced similar moments of feeling empty and
powerless in my own life, in most cases because I wasn't being a
great leader and felt my leadership was only as great as the number
of decisions I made and not the number of people I influenced.
Through the years these moments reawaken in my consciousness
as reminders that I am human and formed from clay. As several of
these moments can replay over and over again in my mind, I have
learned to live with them. Today I believe them to be moments
that remind me always to trust God more than myself and my
decisions and to know that the road to being a great leader is in
the number of people I influence and not the number of decisions
I make in a lifetime.

One such moment came in the form of a phone call from my
family, just after experiencing my burning bush moment to plant
Impact Church. They called to share the news that my father,
who lived more than two thousand miles away from me, was in
the hospital. After traveling to visit him, I felt empty and powerless when I saw him. I knew that the cancer inside of his body
was steadily taking him away, and like every family we prayed for
God's healing touch.

Another painful moment when I chose a "theology of weakness" was when I made a strategic and spiritual decision to say
goodbye to the loving congregation where I served before launching Impact. These good people nurtured me for more than five
years, enabling me to step out on faith to go to a place that didn't
exist outside of my mind and soul. Over the years I have felt empty

and powerless as a pastor sitting in lonely places, contemplating my leadership decisions of the day, the brokenness of our world, and the pressures of ministry. I knew in each of these cases that the number of decisions I made was irrelevant. The most important lesson was how God used my pain, loss, and transitions to influence people for good more than make thousands of decisions.

Shifting from Empty and Powerless

For most of my vocational life, I have described these places and spaces as being empty and powerless. However, I now know that what I was actually experiencing was the divine transformative dynamic of being available. I also believe Moses became available to God in the midst of his questions and concerns. We have all heard the philosophical question "Do you see the glass half-full or half-empty?" There is a slight biblical similarity to this question in the New Testament as Paul is speaking to the Corinthians in 1 Corinthians 13:12, "Now we see a reflection in a mirror; then we will see face-to-face. Now I know partially, but then I will know completely in the same way that I have been completely known." These kind of moments are uncertain, the kind that cause us to wait when we do not fully understand why, what, or how. Yet over time we are able to see that what we're feeling is not emptiness or powerlessness, but power and hope through availability. We seem stuck and hollow, but God is constantly renewing and refreshing us to prepare us for the tremendous blessings of our future, beyond the broken places of our past. Shifting our thoughts from emptiness to availability challenges us to see the world through different and broader lenses, to let go of yesterday in exchange for today.

How available are you right now as a leader?

So, you may be asking, "What does this all mean? How does it apply to my situations?" In life, we all experience "goodbyes" that lead to perceived feelings of emptiness and powerlessness. Like Moses, we as leaders will also find that tough goodbyes are a part of our journeys. Separating from loved ones and from those with whom we share deep connections always creates open places and spaces in our hearts. Historically, some of the greatest goodbyes have been simultaneously awesome and painful. I remember watching the movie *Gone with the Wind* in my fifth-grade class as Rhett Butler told Scarlett O'Hara, "Frankly, my dear, I don't give a damn."[3] Of course, my wonderful teacher muted the sound when Rhett cursed, but the moment and the meaning of the scene stuck with me long after she restored the sound. That scene was one of the most beautiful and painful goodbyes I had ever experienced. As I've mentioned, goodbyes are never easy, but when our perspectives shift, every farewell can create an *available* place and space, rather than an empty and powerless one.

Parting ways with someone creates an internal pruning process that is unavoidable and critical to our strategic and spiritual journeys. We must experience these circumstances as human beings committed to remaining connected to ourselves, God, God's people, and God's promises. Both Moses and the two tribes found their goodbye to be equally hard as all of them were saying yes to their own destinies. The difficulty lay in the loss of friends and significant relationships that they had built over the years. In one single day, Moses, the Gadites, and the Reubenites experienced broken hearts while birthing new opportunities.

I don't want to make the letting-go part of the process seem so easy and swift, because it is not. Letting go causes grief, and grief is never easy but it is possible. Henry Cloud refers to grief in the following way: "The grieving process is a mental and emotional letting go. What that means is to face the reality that it is over, whatever *it* is, and to feel the feelings involved in facing that reality."[4] Wow! Loss and grief are real because it means we have to wake up to the reality that something is missing and something important is no longer with us. This is the hardest part to death and dying—realizing that something that may have been alive and well moments ago is now gone forever. As leaders we will have these experiences more than we can count and more than we want to acknowledge. When people think of pastoral work, they likely believe a pastor's job revolves around three significant areas: preaching sermons and officiating weddings and funerals. Would you believe that out of all of these three primary tasks pastors probably officiate funerals the most? Not the funerals that you would think, but the every day and year funeral of pastoring after looking back over an entire vocational career and seeing how many relationships, committees, toxic influences, and abnormal circumstances they had to bury. These funerals never made it to the graveyard outside but were buried in the heart of the pastor year after year, and over time the pain and grief of loss add up. Numbers 32 shows a very public funeral Moses experienced, but I often wonder how many private funerals Moses experienced that were buried in his heart that scripture never recorded. If you are a leader, you have known many funerals. Some of those funerals have been public but most have been private.

Eventually, Moses could see the future again. Although the details didn't quite produce the same picture as before, the promise remained and it was still real. The promise persisted as long as he continued to be connected, open, and available. The Reubenites and Gadites could also see the future, discovering their personal promises to take the land where they were and not the land God had promised to the Israelites through Moses. Yes, for Moses, the Reubenites, and the Gadites, the contexts of their journeys shifted, but their promises remained.

After the Dust Settles

Shortly after the deal was done, once the tears dried and when the daily routine of managing the Israelites returned, Moses sensed a new calm and energy. This feeling was one that had not moved through his body in a long time. He had felt a calmness after crossing the Red Sea, experiencing God at the burning bush, receiving the commandments on Mount Sinai, and developing a new style of leadership through the urging of his father-in-law, Jethro. Though older now, he could still recall easily the joy, energy, and hope of those moments. It was a unique sensation, more than a feeling; it was really a thought, a "Blessing of the Available Place and Space." God had developed Moses's understanding of this thought over time. From his experience with the Reubenites and Gadites, Moses realized that all the while they were journeying to the promised land, he had been trying to convince all of the Israelites to go to a place to which all of them weren't willing to go. As his shoulders and neck relaxed, Moses understood that he had been carrying a huge weight for many years. Not only had he held the load of leadership, he had been lugging around a whole lot of stress and tension because he never accepted "no" or "turn around" for an answer. He never allowed thoughts of "less than everyone" or any reduction of numbers to enter into his mind. However, after God's leadership development 101, he could let new thoughts and new realities live in his consciousness—that of available place and space.

Are there areas in your life that are cluttered and you need to create available place and space?

As the Reubenites and Gadites moved quickly toward their moving check-off list, Moses had even more choices and decisions to make. With these new available places and spaces, would he allow doubt and fear to creep into his mind? With these vying for his attention, he could've chosen to wonder, "What if others want to leave and I am left alone? What if this emptiness becomes a permanent place in my life forever?" Now, the concept of forever is profound and difficult because no matter how sincere we are when we promise to keep in touch after a goodbye, we can always sense a trace of "forever" wrapped up in our separation. Forever can be a blessing and a curse at the same time, even in Moses's time. He probably thought that the trace of forever in their goodbye was a deeper symbol, one that pointed to his failure as a leader. He continued to recall the lessons from Jethro and tried his best to apply them, but he was at a point beyond those lessons. Jethro never taught him about the "Blessing of the Available Place and Space." Jethro's wisdom ended at how to govern and lead through delegation; it never included how to go through God's leadership development process of subtraction. Life and Jethro switched roles. Moses's father-in-law was no longer his teacher. Now, life and experience would have to deliver Moses's next lessons on leadership. Yes, he had lived a long time, but he was still learning each and every day what it meant to be a leader and how to guide God's people.

What new leadership lesson is God teaching you right now? Is God teaching you subtraction more than addition?

I have come to my own places of realizing that I'd traveled beyond the reach of the wisdom of the communities that first loved and nurtured me. After many bruises and bumps along the way, with life as the instructor, I had to learn the "Blessing of the Available Place and Space." The circumstances I mentioned earlier that left me feeling empty and powerless were such times of learning for me. I chose to understand and accept them and become available to God and life again. While I hoped and prayed that my father would recover from his bout with cancer, he passed away three months before Impact's first worship experience. This was a difficult and joyous season in my life. In one moment I was delivering my father's eulogy, and in the next I was launching a new church, celebrating with our church plant core team of twenty-five people. The words of Job rang true in my life: "The LORD has given; the LORD has taken; bless the LORD's name" (Job 1:21).

Chapter 4

And as you can guess, my family and I said goodbye to the loving faith community so that we could journey into the future with a vision of a church that only existed in our minds and souls. In each of these circumstances, I lost people who were quite dear to me, but God showed me that in every loss I can choose—or not—to be available to the blessings God still has in store for me. These paths have not been easy, but knowing the blessing of the available place and space has made all the difference. Now more than a few years removed from those difficult days, I often reflect and am grateful that my dreams and hopes did not die with my father or the move from the loving congregation.

Another way of considering places that seem empty and lonely is through the lens of a scrapbook. This is a dated terminology but awakened anew in modern society. I believe social media is the new form of scrapbooking. These archives of our lives are filled with aging pictures and the crumbling edges of their interior paper. The emptiness we can feel is like places on the paper that should be filled with photos we cannot find or the ones existing in files on our digital cameras that we keep promising to download one day. The lonely places are our past tragedies and triumphs, our past hopes and failures, our past friends and enemies, our past lovers and haters, our past ups and downs, our past good and bad moments. These places can hold us, grip us, frighten us, and steal our peace, hope, and love. Emptiness and powerlessness can be dangerous when we only view them through past lenses. When we know we have a choice of perspective, the danger becomes a mere shadow. Moses recognized that he had a choice. He could've viewed the tribes' request via the magnifying glass of an empty past place or through the telescopic lens of the future. I am grateful for Moses's story and that he chose to view the experience as one of an available opportunity to receive God's future and not circumstances' past.

Moving Forward

After the final conversation with his elders, Moses rose from his tent and dried his eyes as he pushed fear back, understanding that he turned an almost disastrous moment into a great celebration. He called for the two tribes, to bring them to the center of the community, announcing, "Our friends will be leaving us." The gasps spread quickly and audibly through the crowded space. Before any of the elders could respond, Moses added, "They have been our faith partners, and I support their decision." This gesture may have been one of Moses's finest leadership moments. The time when he faced his fears and his promise, giving permission for others to live into their promises as well. I suspect there were some other tribes who developed a renewed sense of call and hope to possess the land God promised. The choice of the Reubenites and Gadites was an inspiration for most.

To Moses's surprise the people easily followed his lead, celebrating the two tribes as they danced and sang together. When night began to fall on the camp and the roaring fires were glowing, one of Moses's most loyal leaders approached him. He witnessed, "You did a big thing today. I never thought I would live to see this day, when you would be so gracious. Moses, I want you to know that I—we—all of us are with you, and we will make it to the promised land together." Tears welled up again in Moses's eyes as he embraced this elder. They walked together into the approaching sunset. Joshua was nearby, and he joined them on the evening walk. Without any additional words they all considered the same thoughts, ponderings of their future, musings of flowing milk and honey, dreams of triumph and glory. Their thoughts formed smiles on their faces, and they knew the promised land was near.

Questions for Discernment

Available places and spaces may be frightening when we only see them through the lens of loss rather than of gain. We know we have courage and have matured when we can view our greatest losses as postures of being available for God to move in amazing ways in our lives.

1. How do you overcome the feeling of believing that the loneliness will never end once someone leaves or something ends?

2. How do you help people leave with grace?

3. When was the last time something in your life had to decrease before it increased?

Reflection on "Availability" by
Gregory C. Ellison II, PhD

**Associate Professor of Pastoral Care and Counseling,
Candler School of Theology, Atlanta, GA**

Many ages ago, a professor paid a visit to a Japanese Zen master seeking to uncover the secrets of life. Without saying a word, the master teacher began to pour a cup of tea for his guest. He continued pouring until the tea began to spill on the floor. Unable to take it any longer, the professor yelled out, "It is overfull. No more will go in." The Zen master responded, "Like this cup you are full of your own opinions and speculations. How can I show you the [secrets of life] unless you first empty your cup?"[5]

Makes sense, doesn't it? You won't eat if you think you're already full. You won't seek new discoveries if you already know everything. Far too many leaders have cups overfilled with age-old traditions, outdated customs, and naysaying sojourners. With their souls and psyches filled to the brim, these leaders have little room for novel ideas, fresh approaches, and unexpected newcomers bringing the gifts of wisdom.

Earlier in the chapter, Olu Brown noted that after the Reubenites and Gadites departed, Moses "sensed an instant emptiness in the air." This void brought about by missing something or someone of importance left Moses pondering next steps. Brown drew this narrative on emptiness to the present by welcoming the reader into his own void as he wrestled with the illness of his father and his departure from a church family that had nurtured him in ministry. In both Moses's and Brown's situations, emptiness triggered an amalgam of emotions: grief, uncertainty, doubt, fear. Their hearts, their souls were brimming with competing and conflicting emotions.

Here is the paradox. In the times when leaders feel most empty, their cups are actually overfilled with competing and conflicting emotions. To become truly available to the leading of God, Moses and Brown understood the necessity of emptying the cup.

How does one empty the cup? In the case of Moses, he could have chastised the Reubenites and Gadites for their decision to remain in the wilderness. Instead, he celebrated them and gave thanks for the portion of the journey that they had traveled together. To authentically bless the forward trajectory of his beloved, Moses had to untangle the knotted emotions of grief, doubt, and fear. Likewise, Brown had to sort through his own emotions in order to offer a "blessed" goodbye to his ailing father and the faith community that had nurtured his call.

Both of these leaders demonstrate that after the cup is emptied and "the dust settles" from hard, heartfelt goodbyes, a way is opened. With hearts and minds no longer overfilled with competing and conflicting emotions, they were free to let God provide a clarity of vision and concreteness of purpose. Once unburdened and fully available to the direction of God, these leaders became more open to novel ideas, fresh approaches, and unexpected newcomers bringing the gifts of wisdom. In short, they were ready for the promised land.

CONCLUSION

When we started our promised land adventure at the beginning of this book, we reflected on Numbers 32. At the time we did not know the full depth of the spiritual, emotional, and strategic journey of Moses, the Reubenites, and the Gadites. I hope that your time with this story has been transformative, that your reading of the biblical texts going forward will be an opportunity to seek understanding beyond the stories' face value. I pray that you will always dare to peel back the surface of the narratives to touch the emotional drama and tension hidden in the words on the pages. As we become great and deeper leaders, we will share many lessons on leadership; and as we press through them we will be better leaders because of these lessons. Perhaps like Moses you will gain these lessons in the deserts of your life or even in the valley walks of leadership. Kirbyjon Caldwell offers this reflection on growing in our deserts: "We have to go into the desert of our souls before new growth can appear. You must literally go into the desert that exists within you and seek the power of God there. . . . The desert experience will either draw you closer to God or drive you farther away. It's your choice."[1] Here is that word *choice* again. It is up to you to become a great leader and continue to move toward your promise as you give people permission to move toward their promise. Remember the "theology of weakness" by Henri Nouwen doesn't mean you are weak; rather, it means you are acknowledging God is all-powerful. I wish there were an easier road or a road you could quickly travel to grasp the leadership lessons of Moses, but there is only one road, and that road may take you the forty years it took Moses. At times you will be going in a straight line, but most times you will be going in circles. You may not even learn all of the lessons in your lifetime, and like Moses you might only see the promise and entrust it to the next generation. Life and leadership are funny at best but worth living and developing every step of the way.

Moses was a great leader. Reuben and Gad were great tribes. They all wanted to do the right thing, follow their hearts, and submit to the spirit of God. Moses's motivation was that he'd heard God clearly in the desert, meeting God at the burning bush and knowing that his life would never be the same. The Reubenites and the Gadites were inspired to request permission from Moses to leave because they felt, just like Moses, that God had a special promise and allocation for them in the Transjordan. These two tribes were convinced that they could not betray their own destiny for the sake of making the other ten tribes and Moses happy. This increased awareness and enlightenment that Moses, the Reubenites, and the Gadites experienced led to a series of inevitable and difficult conversations.

The most difficult discussion was the initial one. There is always something so frightening about that initial conversation when we make up in our minds that we are going to face the elephant in the room and stop running from reality. It would seem that Moses was the only one to have to face reality, but after further review, both Moses and the two tribes all had to face a new reality and find a way to move forward. The two tribes requested to leave the journey to the promised land in order to remain where they were. Their request forced Moses to face a new reality and make his own spiritual and strategic decisions. The scenes between Moses and the two tribes teach us that life is never as it seems and negotiations are always necessary as we sojourn to our destiny, to the places of promise that God has in store for each of us.

Moses decided to let the Reubenites and the Gadites leave their trek to the promised land because he understood the difference between promise and choice and decisions and influence. Moses clearly knew that God had given him a promise for all of the tribes, but he also realized that God had given the Reubenites and the Gadites a choice and their own destiny to fulfill. Moses was also a great leader not because of the number of decisions he made but because he chose the greater road of influencing people even if it meant leaving some people behind to live with their own choices. The two tribes exercised their choice to live into their own promises from God. And although it broke Moses's heart, he could not be the one standing in their way.

During these conversations, as Moses reached what he thought was his breaking point, a beautiful light consumed him and the space of his tent. This light gave him peace, calming him so that he could push back the thoughts of emptiness and loss in order to embrace the deeper understanding of availability. Moses realized he wasn't losing. Instead he was gaining a new opportunity to trust and follow God. In the end, Moses was faithful to

God, God's promise, and God's people. Moses did not disappoint God, nor did the Reubenites and the Gadites. God loved them all and God gave each of them a promise. I am grateful that they each made the choice to follow God and God's promises. Joshua 1:12-15 tells the end of the story after Moses was gone:

> Then Joshua addressed the Reubenites, the Gadites, and half the tribe of Manasseh: "Remember the command that Moses the LORD's servant gave you: 'The LORD your God will give you rest and give you this land.' Your wives, children, and cattle may remain in the land that Moses has given you on the east side of the Jordan. But all you brave fighters, organized for war, must cross over in front of your fellow Israelites. You must help them until the LORD gives a rest like yours to your fellow Israelites and they too take possession of the land that the LORD your God is giving them. Then you may return and take over the land that belongs to you, which Moses the LORD's servant has given you on the east side of the Jordan."

In the end, the Israelites made it all the way to the promise, and the Reubenites and the Gadites made it to their promise. Remember to keep moving forward and eventually you will make it to your promise because God is with you.

This unique place of parting ways with valuable members of our teams is one that every great leader will experience at some point of her or his journey. In these moments faith is critical: faith in ourselves and faith in God. At these moments we can come to understand that every vision and plan can be tweaked. Sometimes our being too close to the vision prevents us from seeing the light. In these moments we need those who stand at a distance to hold us accountable to the vision. These places are the toughest parts of leading others. These places challenge us with heart-wrenching questions like, "Can you believe in your promise even when others don't believe in it? Can you believe in your promise even when others choose their own promise?" We struggle with the answers to these questions and we battle with self-doubt, a dangerous fuel added to a fire that no fire-resistant chemical can extinguish. Moses asked himself so many questions along the way, especially in the moment when the two tribes asked to leave. Truly, as you lead organizations and people, you will have similarly tough questions—questions about life, questions about what's next, questions about finance, and questions about destiny. These questions are okay as long as they are not detrimental to your soul and do not keep you from moving forward in your journey.

After the Reubenites and Gadites inked their deal with Moses and after Moses finished meeting with all the other Israelite elders, he was alone in his tent. In that moment of solitude and silence, he continued to wonder how well he'd handled the situation. Still, Moses faced the biggest and most challenging leadership question of his journey. This question was an internal one and one that only Moses could answer and only you can answer: "Did I follow God's promise in the midst of so many choices?"

NOTES

1. Beginnings

1. Anugrah Kumar, "Nearly 3 in 4 Pastors Regularly Consider Leaving Due to Stress, Study Finds," *Christian Post*, June 21, 2014, www.christianpost.com/news/nearly-3-in-4-pastors-regularly-consider-leaving-due-to-stress-study-finds-121973/.

2. Olu Brown, 2006 Impact Vision documents.

3. Samuel R. Chand, *Leadership Pain: The Classroom for Growth* (Nashville: Thomas Nelson, 2015).

2. Difficult Conversations

1. Bruce Wilkinson, *The Dream Giver: Following Your God-Given Destiny* (Colorado Springs: Multnomah, 2009).

2. Samuel R. Chand, *Leadership Pain: The Classroom for Growth* (Nashville: Thomas Nelson, 2015), iv.

3. W. A. Elwell and B. J. Beitzel, *Baker Encyclopedia of the Bible* (Grand Rapids: Baker Book House, 1988), 2099–2100.

4. Kirbyjon Caldwell, *Gospel of Good Success: A Road Map to Spiritual, Emotional and Financial Wholeness* (New York: Simon & Schuster, 1999), 107.

3. Your Promise, My Choice

1. Andy Stanley, *Next Generation Leader: Five Essentials for Those Who Will Shape the Future* (Colorado Springs: Multnomah, 2003), 53.

2. Robert Frost, "The Road Not Taken," www.poetryfounda tion.org/resources/learning/core-poems/detail/44272. This poem is in the public domain.

4. Availability

1. Henri Nouwen, *Finding My Way Home: Pathways to Life and the Spirit* (New York: Crossroad, 2001), 42.

2. See Jim Collins, *Good to Great* (New York: HarperBusiness, 2001).

3. *Gone with the Wind*, directed by Victor Fleming (1939; Culver City, CA: Selznick International Pictures).

4. Henry Cloud, *Necessary Endings: The Employees, Businesses, and Relationships That All of Us Have to Give Up in Order to Move Forward* (New York: HarperCollins, 2010), 213.

5. Paul Reps, *Zen Flesh, Zen Bones: A Collection of Zen and Pre-Zen Writings* (Rutland, VT: Charles E. Tuttle, 2000), 19.

Conclusion

1. Kirbyjon Caldwell, *The Gospel of Good Success: A Road Map to Spiritual, Emotional and Financial Wholeness* (New York: Simon & Schuster, 1999), 75.

Made in United States
North Haven, CT
30 March 2023

34802602R00055